MW01027621

The Pimp's Bible
OR
The Sweet Science of Sin

RESEARCH ASSOCIATES SCHOOL TIMES PUBLICATIONS

The Pimp's Bible

Alfred Bilbo Gholson

Published by

Research Associates School Times Publications

Distributed by

Frontline Distribution Int'l, Inc.
751 East 75th Street
Chicago, IL 60619 USA
773-651-9888

CHICAGO • JAMAICA • LONDON
REPUBLIC of TRINIDAD and TOBAGO
CARIBBEAN

Published by
Research Associates School Times
Publications/
Frontline Distribution Int'l, Inc.
751 East 75th Street
Chicago, IL 60619
Tel: (773) 651-9888
Fax: (773) 651-9850
E-mail: Frontlinebooks@prodigy.net

ISBN 0-94839-079-4

Publisher's Note

This book - The Pimp's Bible was very difficult to publish. The editing of it was a very complex job, mainly because the book was written in a strong street language style.

Hence, the intricate task at hand was;

1.) To clean up the grammar;
2.) To tighten up the punctuation;
3.) To re-structure the author's classy style; or the flamboyant way in which Bilbo tells these real stories.

The first person who was recommended for the task of editing, failed in her endeavor. Thus, we at Frontline decided to undertake this responsibility in-house. Camille Richins, who is and would always be very dear to me did a great part of the work, along with your servant. Hence, the Pimp's Bible is finally here, read it, and comprehend: *The Sweet Science Of Sin.*

Give Thanks,

Sekou Tafari, July '97

The Pimp's Bible

or

The Sweet Science of Sin

by
Alfred "Bilbo" Gholson

RESEARCH ASSOCIATES SCHOOL TIMES PUBLICATIONS

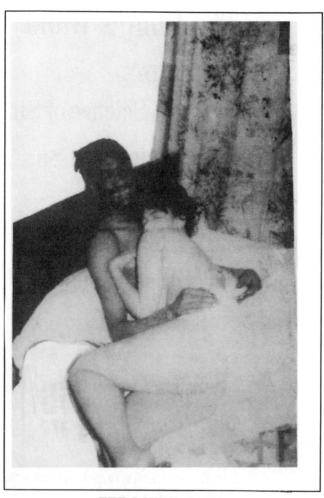

THE LOVING PIMP

The Pimp's Bible
OR
The Sweet Science of Sin

AFRICA'S FINEST

CHINA'S FINEST

MEXICO'S FINEST

AMERICA'S FINEST

PREFACE

The **Sweet Science of Sin** is not a book of " *This is My Story or "My Life as a Pimp*," but it is a documentary.

Its purpose is to serve as a guideline of the true facts and facets of the pimp and prostitute lifestyle. This information was previously unknown to the average American citizen. This book was written in 1986 and probably needs a bit of updating due to the increase use of crack cocaine and gang activities. I truly believe it is a needed piece of information for the general public.

Life is a constant struggle for one to better oneself in the society in which he or she lives.

Unfortunately, I lived in a society of pimps, whores, prostitutes, drug pushers, drug users, robbers, burglars, cutthroats, and bandits. Love me or hate me, it does not matter because pimping was not my choice.

If I had to choose my profession, I would have been like Sugar Ray Robinson, the boxer. You must realize it was God's choice. Someone had to pimp so that the whores and prostitutes could have companionship, love and happiness.

I must have set a blazing trail in the world of pimps and prostitutes, by simultaneously dealing with 23 *"ladies of the evening and daughters of the night"*.

I had the fruits of a pimp's success for forty years and

could not have asked for anything better.

Now, at this age in my life I have nothing material to show. There are some millionaires that have confronted the same fate as I have and ended up as bums, alcoholics, dope fiends, or even committed suicide. But, I am strong and have enough sweet memories (which is all I have left) to carry me to my grave.

Thanks for the sweet memories.
Alfred 'Bilbo' Gholson.

A VINTAGE PIMP, CHARLES (BABY) BELL ONLY DEALS WITH WHITE GIRLS

BABY BELL

In 1920 there was plenty of bootlegging, killing and pimping going on. While G-Men were trying with all their might to catch those doing wrong; while Al Capone was painting the town red, the stool-pigeons listened closely to hear what was being said.

There was one such guy who didn't have to do any dirt, all he had to do was play behind his white women's skirts. He was a real pimp and everyone could tell, because whenever he walked into any place, they cried out, "there is ***BABY BELL!***" With a blond on one arm and a brunette on the other, the first words to come out of his mouth were "hello brother!"

Bell said there were two things that he didn't like, being broke and anything that was ugly and black! He loved white women and made them rob white men. When the law paid him a visit he'd tell them to "hurry back again!"

He would drive to **Club De Lisa** in his big Pierce-Arrow car, walk in with a white woman on each arm and lay thousands of dollars on the bar. He would turn around to see who he knew and yell out, "Am I the only ***nigger pimp*** in here with some white snow?"

The crowd laughed when he laughed and the bartenders smiled when he smiled, for they were getting some generous tips all the while.

The black girls have a *backyard* to play in while the white girls have the *whole world* and this is just as faithful as an oyster giving me a pearl each day.

Baby Bell died a horrible death; one day while in Washington Park he placed a pistol in his mouth and his world suddenly went dark!

DECLARATION

The text of the *"Sweet Science of Sin"* was written with no intention of offending, sneering, degrading, mocking or making anyone feel uncomfortable; especially the oral and anal lovers or drug addicts. I have friends, associates and relatives from all walks of life who only make this piece of work more marketable and controversial.

I wrote this book realizing that each snow flake that falls from the sky has a different design; just as each lifestyle is as individual as a fingerprint.

Some people do not like doctors, lawyers, firemen, policemen, gays, pimps or prostitutes. Some don't even like God and he wakes them each morning.

But a high-class pimp loves everyone - that is what makes him so special. Just ask yourself, "Is a whore or prostitute entitled to life, love and the pursuit of happiness?"

On the following page you will find a poem entitled, *"The Pimp"* which I would like you to read and reread.

The "Sweet Science of Sin" is perhaps the only guideline that you will ever find, describing a pimp because only three people understand the pimp - and that's God, a whore, and another pimp...

Thank you sincerely and I hope you enjoy this book!

Alfred 'Bilbo' Gholson.

THE PIMP

White men started macking and gigoloing
after the writing of the Bible
But when the Black man started pimping
Didn't have a title.

At the freeing of the slaves
Black men were labeled Wimps
But after a few years of freedom
That was immediately changed to Pimp.

There was no such thing as Black prostitution
or pimping
Until after the freeing of the slaves
YOU SEE, that's why the Pimp game
Is the Black man's creation.

Wearing their three-piece suits
and their diamonds stick pins,
It looked like the Black man
was about to get in!

They started buying their own land and property
and driving their shiny cars
Laughing, loving, playing with the ladies
and smoking their big cigars.

Now the white man can gigolo and he can mack
But when it comes to real pimping

He will have to take lessons from a Black.

There are multitudes of people
who will never, never know
Because none understand a pimp
But God, another pimp and a whore.

The pimp is a distinctive character
with an exceptional intellect
He possesses the ability
to deal with the most difficult task
and does it with the greatest of ease
and each and everyone of his lady friends
are very much pleased.

It is accepted that it is difficult
for the world to understand
but God made the pimp
So the whore and the prostitute
Could have a MAN!

This poem was written by:
Alfred 'Bilbo' Gholson.

FOREWORD

Please do not misconstrue this book as a source of encouragement to the youth of the present or the future. The purpose of the book is to enlighten readers of the true activities on the subject. By no means is this book written as a vehicle to glamorize or upgrade this infamous profession. We sincerely hope and pray that it will serve as a discouragement and help many more minds, particularly the young uneducated, uncultivated ones, into constructive channels which will assist in his or her becoming a productive citizen.

We hope it will serve as a needed dose of information on the subject of pimps and prostitutes. Since the days of Mary Magdalene and Jezebel the negative side of life's record has been playing. So, let us just turn it over for a while and see how it sounds. On January 30, 1986, the popular *Oprah Winfrey Show* had several brothel *"house madams"* as guests who brought out several good and valid points about the life. One had even written a book entitled *Call Me Madam*. Also on that show there was one ex-Modern-Day pimp who older Chicagoans should know very well, namely, Bishop Magic Juan. He stated that he was once the greatest pimp in the world but now he is working for God. One of the older madams on the show did not believe he was legitimate and accused him of being a con artist. But that's because pimps and house madams have an intense vendetta against one another. They are serious competitors. *(In chapter 1X you will read about The Pimps' and House Madams' Vendetta).*

The show provided some facts, facets, and events of the past, present and no doubt the future. It is no longer a shadow in the pimps and prostitutes eyes why the general society feels and thinks the way they do about the word *"pimp"*. If the viewers of the Oprah Winfrey Show and the movie-goers observe the dress of our Modern-Day pimp, then you can hardly blame society's opinion.

If the *"professors"* and *"deans"* of the pimp world knew how they were being portrayed, they would virtually turn over in their graves. A high-class pimp would never portray himself in such a fashion. With just a little research on the high-class pimps' attire, you will find that it is a well known and established fact that the high-class pimps have won many trophies and awards for their excellent taste in fashion, automobiles, non-gaudy jewelry and have always being regarded as elegant dressers. Most of the pimps can take credit for being trend setters. Being envy only to the manner in which Hollywood paints the picture the naive public has no choice than to believe the big red hats with the sky-scraping feathers, the multi-colored suits, the platform shoes, the ruffled blouse-like shirts, the mink coat tossed around his shoulders, dark glasses, a walking cane and a custom-made automobile looking like a parade float.

That may impress the younger generation or give society to another Bozo to laugh at but it is a high insult to the few higher class pimps that are still around.

Cary Grant, Adolph Menjou, Edward G. Robinson, Humphrey Bogart, James Cagney, and Frank Sinatra would all have to take a back seat when it came to matching a "king" pimp in his manner of dress. Higher class pimps admired cer-

tain movie stars and none of the above-mentioned would dare
dress in the fashion that the movie makers portray as a pimp.

The fashion designers and the merchants only make those
type of clothing for the people of color, minorities, i. e., Native
Americans, Puerto Ricans, Mexicans and African Americans,
and only the uneducated, dumb ones buy and wear that crap.
A common laborer can buy houses, cars, diamonds, and all the
other expensive items but that still does not put him in certain
classes—such as that of a first-class pimp.

Ex-Classy Pimp
Alfred 'Bilbo' Gholson.

STACY AND TWO FAST STEPPING WHORES

INTRODUCTION

With forty years' of experience, a nationwide survey, and living in the midst of thousands of pimps and prostitutes have provided ex-classy pimp Alfred "Bilbo" Gholson the best opportunity to get the truth from his interview. What prostitutes would tell a newspaper reporter or a television talk show host for a few dollars is different from what they would tell a man of Smith's reputation and background.

Alfred "Bilbo" Gholson, an ex-high class pimp and operator of several first-class brothels, has come to the conclusion that society is so up in the air concerning the lifestyles of the pimps and prostitutes. The negative side of every situation is always first to be recognized as truth and believed by the negative.

The undesirables in the pimp world, (low-class pimps and prostitutes) have always been a keg of dynamite to explode. Unfortunately, they are not qualified to get in the places where real prostitution money flows and they break any and all codes and rules of the profession, while trying to survive. The worse whores, i.e., street walkers, flatbacks, outlaws, chippies and drug addicts are held responsible for the vile conduct. But society will sweep it under the rug by saying "all of them are the same."

It seems the root of the confusion stems from the ignorance of not being able to distinguish the difference between the good Indians and the bad ones. It would appear senseless for black society to get overwhelmingly upset because a white nut rapes a black woman and blames all whites and the same applies to white society when a black nut rapes a white woman. Each individual should make their own bed the way he or she likes to sleep.

Al Capone's (right) signature is on the Valentine delivered to archrival George Bugs Moran's garage

Alfred "Bilbo" Gholson, has been involved in the pimp world since he was 20 years old. He believes that he has all the answers because he has been asked all the questions concerning this topic. One thing he says that is certain, is that "today's pimps could not shine a boot of yesterday's pimp."

Any man who would put a hypodermic needle in a child's arm loaded with heroin, cocaine or any other form of narcotics is considered a very low level of scum. Whether he's a pimp or a preacher. He could not look you in the eye and say he is or was a high-class pimp. In the 1940's, there weren't many drug addicts around. To allow your woman to shoot drugs was a no-no, and any man who permitted such was looked upon with disdain.

High-class mackmen and pimps have always been essential to the public, giving them what they wanted and needed, especially during the Great Depression. This is in the same respect as the politicians, judges, policemen and soup line recipients loved, admired and adored the late Al Capone and considered his criminal activities as competitive.

He gave the public what they asked for. Had they given him a legal liquor license, he would have no need to bootleg. Had they not disrupted the houses of ill repute, Prostitution would have been legal. Many of today's laws need to be desperately revamped. At this point in time, liquor is legal and in some states Prostitution is legal and is becoming more and more accepted each day.

So all the killings in the "roaring twenties" were unnecessary when whiskey and prostitution were to be legalized anyway. Al Capone was not the type of individual who preyed on innocent people —he used them but he didn't misuse them. His problem came from his competitors, his own kind, when they came to take what belonged to him. He took millions of dollars

and he put back millions of dollars to feed and shelter
the poor and hungry.

The pimps and the prostitutes have always been
last on the ladder and so has American society when it
comes to facing life head on and looking at it as it is.
Regardless of how society accepts or looks upon a pimp
or prostitute, there is a high class pimp and prostitute.
However, the only one that the public has the opportunity to see is the modern day pimp on screen in the
olden days. From prohibition until the later 1970's, the
high class pimp and mackmen owned all the classy night
spots and fancy supper clubs. Had it not been for these
underworld type characters, the public would not have
had any place to go, especially the Blacks.

Thirty five percent of the public were Christians,
legitimate business people, and white collars who were
not going to invest in these types of establishments. On
the other hand, thirty-five percent were mackmen,
pimps and underworld figures who backed the women
and booze and the other thirty percent were the patrons.

In our four leading cities, New York City, Chicago, Los Angeles, and Detroit, the syndicate has always called the shots. New York's famed *Cotton Club*
and *Small's Paradise Birdland* were backed by mack-
men as were many top Chicago night clubs. *The Toast
of the Town, DuSable Lounge, Circle Bar, The Crown
Propeller*, were all owned or operated by a mackman
or high-class pimp. In Detroit, *the Black and Tan Club,
Cozy Corner, Twenty-Grand, The Fame Show Bar, and
The Frolic Show Bar*, were all owned or operated by
mackmen or high-class pimps.

In Cleveland, Scatter-Brain owned his share of
supper clubs and night spots, backed by White Chicago
Mackmen.

In the 1960's, this was followed by the later generation—*DeVille Lounge* owned by Lawrence Hill; *Pep-*

per Mint Lounge owned by Tommy Walker; *Tiger Lounge* owned by Cubie; Bilbo's *Cimmaron Strip,* and *High Chapperal* owned by Alfred "Bilbo" Gholson.

In those days, it was a common thing to see celebrities, doctors, lawyers, politicians, athletes and boxing champions and their wives or girlfriends, mingling together. Ladies of the evening and daughters of the night flaunted their beauty and furs at the same level that the professionals' wives and lady friends flaunted theirs.

This side of the record plays a different tune. It shows that the undesirables were really the desirables. Before the great **Cab Calloway** became famous, he mentioned in his autobiography, *"Minnie the Moochie and Me"*, that in the early 1920's he accepted $200.00 a week and lived in a brothel. Fatha' Earl Hines in his autobiography, *"The World of Earl Hines"*, stated that he admired the pimps and the Pierce Arrow automobiles that they drove (Rolls Royce today). Even the great **Billy Ekstein** was no stranger to the pimp life.

Take a look on Page 40 in the autobiography of "Black *Chicago*" by Dempsey L. Travis, there you will get a better understanding of how different things are presently.

If all pimps and prostitutes were as notorious as society makes them out to be, then why would society care to rub shoulders with them? The only thing that puzzled the professionals is how could these people afford to live in the same fashion as they?

High-class pimps are considered "King Pimps" among their peers. In a king pimp's domain he is not to be frowned upon.

But society has a strange twist; it looks at a King Pimp in the same respect that they look at a king snake. In Arizona, Utah, Wyoming and many other states, there are severe penalties for killing a king snake - who is merely on earth to protect innocent people from the worst kinds.

However, ignorance intervenes to the extent that a multitude won't allow themselves to dig beyond the surface to seek out the real truth or learn the difference between the good snakes and the bad snakes. To them, a snake is a snake. As to that group of unknowledgeable, a pimp is a pimp, - that is a grave mistake.

It has been said that there are 52 weeks in a year, 52 cards in a deck of playing cards, 52 ways of playing solitaire and 52 versions of pimps. You will find them and their definitions in later chapters. The profile of a King Pimp can be found in Chapter 4.

There is a king in every field and only two will remain forever and that is the King of Heaven and the King of Hell.

One picture means more than a thousand words.

TABLE OF CONTENTS

TOPICS IN THE SWEET SCIENCE OF SIN

*THE CRIMES THAT UPPER-CLASS PIMPS DO
NOT COMMIT*

*THE CRIMES THAT UPPER-CLASS PIMPS
WOULD NOT DARE COMMIT*

*THE CRIMES THAT UPPER-CLASS PIMPS
WOULD NOT EVEN THINK OF*

*WOULD THE REAL SCUM OF THE EARTH,
PLEASE STAND UP*

*IS IT: WOMEN KILLERS, CHILD KILLERS, CHILD
MOLESTERS, RAPISTS, HIRED KILLERS, DRUG
PEDDLERS, PIMPS, PROSTITUTES OR IS IT
<u>AMERICA'S SOCIETY?</u>*

**LADIES OF THE EVENING
FLAUNTING THEIR FURS AND JEWELRY**

CHAPTER 1
FACTS AND FACETS

I often count my blessings and wonder why God spared me while most of my pimp peers just seem to have fallen by the wayside. Through jealousy or simply the life they lived, many were killed. Whenever one reaches his pinnacle in his/her chosen field, jealousy begins to swell. Jealousy is a man's or woman's rage.

The high class pimps could well afford to drive around in new luxury automobiles year after year, dressing in the latest fashions, having excess money to spend and a stable of lovely ladies getting in line to be with him.

It's enough to disturb the average layman who works hard every day and still can't have these type of advantages. But I have no doubt in my mind that my friends who died of what was considered natural causes, were really only the results of cocaine. They all indulged highly, in those days, in what was claimed not to be habit forming, but would help you to perform better sexually and stay up longer hours without sleep.

But I pride myself in being an excellent listener but not a very good follower. I seldom indulged but then when I did, it was only to be sociable.

The pimps that I refer to were all high-class and rode the crest of a pimp's success. During the golden days when "pimps were pimps," there was only a handful of female addicts around.

Prostitutes felt it was an honor to boast and brag that she was the first whore to buy her man a new automobile and brought home the most money. Whatever costly automobile that was in demand, expensive wardrobes, jewelry, homes or farms, and lavishly-furnished apartments, were a must. Real prostitutes looked upon it as a pleasure to see who could bring their pimp the most and the best. My version of pimps and prostitutes is previously untold. The naivety of society is shocking. Some of the myths that surround a pimp is outrageous. The following are only a few examples:

1. The pimp takes a whore's money.

Common sense would permit any positive thinking individual to know that there is no need to take it. Why would he have to take her earnings when she brings it home with joy? It could be very simple for her to take another route if that was her choice. But to her, it's a pleasure and a privilege to give her money to her pimp.

2. Women that say they wouldn't give a man money.

One can be guaranteed that the only ones that you would hear say that do not have any money, or is not qualified to get any. The queen pays the king honor and respect. (Although this is a new era).

3. All pimps engage in oral lovemaking.

That's ridiculous. Society would be utterly surprised to know how many higher classed pimps would never entertain the thought of putting his mouth where his or other penises penetrate. The one who advocate this lie is probably a heavy indulger and trying to rectify himself or believe that's what makes a pimp tick. According to Dr. A. L. Braxton, oral sex and any other types of sex is alright if both parties are consenting adults. At certain pimp meetings, which a layman would never have the opportunity to attend, this discussion often comes up and it is always a big joke.

Higher classed pimps wouldn't dare let his women become equal with him. He believes that any man that has oral love with his woman is her human douche bag.

High class pimps are under the impression that a woman's body accepts so much filth during a month's time, that nature forces a cleaning out period once a month.

Doctors say it's acceptable but the doctors aren't God and most high classed pimps have their own opinion about it.

All subjects not found in the Holy Bible will always remain a mystery to the multitude of laymen. The words pimp, mackman, gigolo, procurer, oral sex, prostitution cannot be found in the Holy Bible (you will find whore, but not prostitute). *The Sweet Science of Sin* is your guideline on these subjects.

4. All pimps are cold hearted.

Granted, there are some very cold-hearted pimps but they are not nearly as cold hearted as some members of "normal" society. A cold-hearted pimp may trick, force or intimidate a naive young girl into prostitution or trick her into drugs. But, a cold-hearted layman will get upset about a woman's body and kill the whole family—children and all. What could be colder than that?

5. Pimps are lazy and don't want to work.

Well, pimping is his job and a pimp works. He constantly deals with seven or more female minds, when the average layman cannot deal with one. If anyone thinks it's not work, let them try it.

6. The pimp forces the prostitute into prostitution.
There is no force necessary when it comes to professional pimping. The pimp is as essential to the prostitute as the king is to his queen, the executive to

his secretary, the doctor to his nurse, the husband to his wife, and the president to the first lady.

All six of the myths you have just read are outrageous, derogatory, low down and degrading and are some of the biggest lies that have ever been told. Society speaks of respectability and morals, but when it comes to money and sex, society throws morals and respectability out the window.

In no sense of the world is this book defending the type of pimps who display such degrading, disgraceful, and tasteless conduct upon others who detest what they are doing more so than society does.

Negativity always rears its ugly head first but positivity is good and good always wins in the end. In chapter IV you will find five of the worst types of pimps. Those kind of pimps and laymen kill the entire family or sexually and physically abuse their sons and daughters and therefore should be tarred and feathered. Some of the things I have witnessed would be very difficult for the average person to envision or believe. The worst types of pimp have done some things that were downright cruel, brutal, shameful and pure wasteful. Those types of pimps or people are very insecure and they must find someone that is weaker than they are, so they prey on the young, naive and sometimes even children.

I have realized how the American society looks at the pimp and prostitute situation but I plead, please do not blame all presidents of the United States because of the "Watergate Scandal." As the world turns, there will be many more such subjects unraveled. The United States is my homeland and I dread that it always comes in last in most conversations. Fashion, dances, tongue and other happenings dominate the common mind.

Great Britain is far ahead of the United States in almost everything but nuclear power and wealth. Prostitution is legal there, as long as it is not forced.

Pimps with class do not entertain the thought of misusing intimidation, life-threatening talk, or coercing a female into prostitution. A prostitute is usually going to survive the way that she sees fit and usually that trust is love.

There is no love like a pimp's love.

Some may wonder what is so special about a pimp's love? A pimp's love is genuine. He does not like being too lax in the use of the word *love*. He refuses to rush in where angels fear to tread. When a pimp tells a woman that he loves her, that alone makes his love both real and rare.

What is a pimp? A pimp is just the opposite of the layman. He can help a woman who is stumbling in the dark see the light again. He brings the best out in the worst of women. Where the layman makes a human bitch out of her, the pimp makes a prostitute out of her. The layman tricks her out of free sex, the pimp teaches her to keep right on enjoying sex but to stick her hand out first, because it does not make any real sense to keep giving away something that is good enough to sell. It is to the layman's advantage to teach a girl that if she accepts money for her body then she is a prostitute. But he also holds that if she does not get marriage or money she is a "human bitch."

As long as the layman can get sex free, he will never give her marriage or money. The pimp teaches her about money and if she has sex to give away she should give it to her pimp, manager, husband and the surplus should be for sale. This is the biggest vendetta that a layman has with a pimp. The sight of a pimp to a layman is like the cross to a Dracula. The layman despises the pimp.

The pimp also teaches the prostitute how to take advantage of the wonderful gifts that God has bestowed upon her. God blessed her with a stick to fight with, which is ten times stronger than a man's stick ever dared to be.

Society wonders what makes a pimp tick. But it is a well known and established fact that the world is a stage and everyone plays a part, trying to win an Oscar. The pimps and prostitutes world is just like in the movies, the actress is the star and the manager is the producer. Her fans are her audience, but they must pay to see the show.

In prostitution, the whore is the star and her tricks are her audience. Her man is her pimp and her audience must pay before she performs.

How can anyone explain a pimp or the field of pimping and have never participated in it. Hearsay is not acceptable. The pimp has always been the tenth wonder of the world. Only three people understand a pimp — God, his women, and another pimp.

High class pimps are distinctive characters with an exceptional, natural intellect and also possess the ability to deal with the most difficult of tasks confronting them with style and ease. Society is unconsciously selfish. They don't realize just how important a pimp is to a prostitute. They are also God's creation and God created a mate for each and everyone. What would the prostitute do for companionship if God had not created the pimp? Is she not entitled to love, life, and the pursuit of happiness?

It seems as though the experts are hesitant to bring out the roots of the pimp. Who is he? From where did he originate? Why is he on earth? Are they afraid to bring out the true meaning of a pimp? Or is it that they don't have a guideline on him? It is amazing how frightening, powerful and intriguing this tiny word

PIMP is.

One of the reasons *The Sweet Science of Sin* was written was to explain the true meaning of the pimp. Since there are no available guidelines on the pimp, God has blessed me with the wisdom and ability to elaborate and make an attempt to enlighten the people on this Planet Earth of the true meaning of a pimp.

Almost every infamous facet of life is coming out of the closet, with the exception of the pimp. There was a time when it was a disgrace for a female's ankle to be exposed. Can you imagine how these same people of that generation would react, if they existed in the world today? How would they react if they witnessed women in string bathing suits, or even in the *Hustler* or *Playboy* magazines where the women are pictured nude.

What could be worse than the lesbian epidemic, homosexuality, child molestation, child pornography, pregnancy out of wedlock, live-in relationships, female impersonators, bare-breasted waitresses, Catholic priests being indicted on young- boys molestation. Even incest is becoming popular. What in the past was looked upon as repulsive is now top rating for television viewing and box office sellout at the movie houses. The only subject that is still lingering in the dark is the **PIMP**.

I recently heard a talk show host ask a priest, " how can you give counselling on marriage and you have never been married?"

The priest's reply was, "I didn't realize certain things until after I got married.

These are some of the same questions that are still hiding in the dark concerning a pimp. How can he be judged by society?

My biggest fear, as far as the naive society is concerned, is that society will not close the gates to the barn until the horses have gotten out. Young innocent girls

need protection NOW. There are some brutal things
that occur in the vicious circle of the jungle and most of
it happen to young girls and teenagers. There is a solution for the young, innocent girls. But instead of society seeking the aide of a professional ex-pimp to really
explain the do's and don'ts and the best steps to take
toward avoiding certain foul situations, they search for
answers from those who don't know.

The real problem with this generation of so-
called pimps is they never had anyone to pass down
the real knowledge, the real know-how. As a rule,
knowledge is passed down from generation to generation, but after drugs got such a firm grip on the young
generation, the old timers backed away and the pimps
had to fend for themselves.

Introduction to drugs, giving birth to babies for
the purpose of black market, step fathers beating babies to death, murder of parents by children zonked
out on drugs, these type of things were rare in the good
old days. Now is the "pipe" era, and it is said to be
worse than the heroin era.

There was a time when Blacks were reluctant
to commit certain crimes due to religious beliefs, but
the new forms of drugs have affected that reasoning.

Each generation will have their share of pimps
and prostitutes. As one generation makes its debut in
that profession one can detect the older ones fading out.
The time has come for the old to say good-bye and good-
luck. But if I was pimping today, dead whores would
turn over in their graves if they even thought that I was
being treated like the modern day pimp, and the old
ones who are still out here would come out of the
woodworks to protest.

The President of the United States, the heavyweight boxing champion, and other influential millionaires would come nearer to giving up their titles or positions than a king pimp would come to giving up his.

It does not matter or worry high class pimps what society thinks of them; it is what they think of society. High class pimps live similar to the lion. True, he is the laziest animal in the jungle but he is still *king of the jungle*. He is a form of a pimp. It is the lioness who is the hunter and the vicious killer in the pursuit for food. The lioness has to give because the lion has to live. He lays in the den and plays with the cubs while she hunts her victims.

Since it has been confirmed by a professor of this infamous subject, that there are 52 versions of pimps, there must be 52 ways for their women to support them. The question has been asked a million times, " If a woman deals with a pimp, does she have to be a whore?"

By no means, **NO.** Good looking, tall, charismatic, young pimps are wanted by some of the wealthiest women across the nation. Housewives support pimps, just as the husbands support the prostitutes.

When men start realizing that women are just as human as they are, it will be a better world in which to live. Some of the less fortunate women, who were not born with a beautiful face and body or with a silver spoon in their mouth are not in demand by tricks. No one wants to marry them and sit them down, so she learns to do something other than sell her body. You may not have a pretty face or a lovely body but don't forget everyone has a brain. Some women resort to their brain department.

Of the 52 versions of pimps, 35 percent prefer not to be called pimps. The other 15 percent are for real; they have nothing to hide. Any man who accepts money from a female is a pimp, because no "man" accepts money from females but pimps.

The women of today never cease to amaze me. They are the easiest prey in the world for the *masked* Pimp to play on. She may think she is getting away from the pimp but runs right into his grasp, as long as he does not call himself a pimp. The only pimps that today's females can recognize is the 15 percent that do not mind being recognized. They want it known.

It has been said that you cannot pimp a lie. Pimps that are genuine refuse to stay in the closet, they flaunt themselves, and want the world to know that they are mates to the unwanted because they also feel unwanted by this hypocritical society.

In the pioneer days when red-blooded men were men, during the covered wagon days when macho men would go and stay for months at a time digging for gold, it was an insult for women to offer any assistance other than stay at home and take care of their children until their men returned home— but that was long, long ago.

"Why do you put that sign on your back Bilbo, letting everyone know that you are pimp? You can get more women to come your way if you fool them. You will have their money and be gone before they wake up," commented my hypocrite pimp friend.

I answered, "I am for real, you are a hypocrite pimp. I have nothing to hide from anybody. You cannot pimp a successful lie. I am a real pimp pal. You see, you work and you don't have the time to put into this game the way I have."

There is some bad in the best of us and some good in the worst of us. Corruption is contagious, from the chief executive down to the pimps and prostitutes. There are some undesirables in every walks of life. Let us just get together and weed them out. If society thinks it can escape pimps and prostitutes, they are in for a big surprise because they are all around — prostitution has a thousand faces.

CHAPTER 2
PIONEERS OF PROSTITUTION

Since Adam and Eve, sin has flourished. Women of the Bible such as Jezebel, the daughter of Ethbaal, the King of the Zidonians, was one of the pioneers of prostitution and committed many sinful activities yet by the grace of God, was forgiven and washed clean of her sins.

Mary Magdalene was a prostitute. She had sinned but was saved by the love of God through the love of Jesus. To prove her love and appreciation of Jesus, Mary washed his feet with the tears from her eyes and dried them with the hair of her head. She was saved from her sinful ways to forever walk in peace. She became a follower of Jesus and was said to be the last to leave the cross after his crucifixion.

The habit of trading sex for survival was adopted by the poor village women. Most village women were poor, but there were some outstanding consequences in that they no longer wanted to eat the crust of bread thrown to the ground by the wealthy. As Scarlet O'Hara was to say later in the movie version of Gone With the Wind, " I may lie, steal, and cheat, but I'll never go hungry again."

Sarah and Abraham accepted Hagar, a young beautiful lass, as a servant. Sarah, Abraham's beloved wife, was unable to bear children, so she convinced Hagar to lay with Abraham to bear them a child. After this was done and over a period of time two children were born to Abraham and Hagar. After the birth of the second son, Sarah became jealous of Hagar and chased her to the desert.

Hagar was 22-years-old and a beautiful female

specimen with flaming red hair that fell below her der-riere and a body that would have excelled Venus De Milo's. She was an extremely poor village girl who was paid back-door visits by the village men. The affluent men in the society also began to shower her with spices, gold, rubies, diamonds and many other valuable gifts.

Other poor village women began to notice Hagar's sudden change and prosperity. They turned on her; "she had sinned and should be stoned to death" was their cry. Whenever Hagar was seen in public, there was always one who would toss a stone and turn his or her head. Hagar became immune to stones and nothing could stop her from the new way of life she had discovered. The high priest, the King's men and men from all around the countryside, continued to pay Hagar back-door visits, since they did not want to be seen with her in public. Hagar had almost as many jewels and other valuables as a queen; however, in the village society, she was considered lower than a serpent's belly-a daughter of the night, a harlot, a whore, and if a man was seen associating with her, he was considered a whore monger.

Nevertheless, men still came in droves to trade jewels for sex with the Sophia Loren type Hagar. Her beauty was irresistible. Men could not resist her charms. Hagar was very wealthy but could not attend any of the festivals, balls, or functions that the villagers presented ever so often. Hagar lived a lonely life and lived to be quite old. She died alone but she left a curse behind her. After her death, many of the same poor villagers realized that they no longer had to be hungry. What society thought of them did not feed them nor clothe their families. It was a tragedy for Hagar to die without a mate. Had mack-men, gigolos, or pimps been discovered, she would have had true love and compan-ionship.

This author thinks that since then, God has decided to make a match for all of his creations. Did God's creations live without a mate? Jezebel, Mary Magdalene and Hagar became legends because they were the pioneers of prostitution.

Women with burning desires to trade sex for gold were popping up all over. They were coming out of the woodwork. You could buy three chippies for $200 worth of gold dust. (Back then prostitutes were called chippies.) In the fledgling part of the US, during the turn of the century, men were hungry for the chippies, until the businessmen came with enough money to make a business out of the chippies by opening up whore-houses and letting them clean themselves up and feel somewhat like somebody.

Lots of other business men thought of the idea but usually someone would always seem to have the choice spots staked. They made big offers, intimidated, tricked, and cajoled trying to buy-out or frighten-out the saloon or whorehouse owner.

Occasionally, a special good whore would drift through and put something new on the businessmen's mind and she would end up the madam of the whorehouse. The businessman then would be called a Mack-man today.

A PIMP'S ATTIRE OF YESTERYEARS

CHAPTER 3
BIRTH OF THE MACK-MAN, GIGOLO, PIMP AND PROCURER

Around the turn of the century business-minded men with money made a business out of chippies. These mack-men built saloons, and places called cat-houses, whore-houses, houses of pleasure and brothels.

It was strictly business to the mack-men. They were not interested in the girls themselves, only for the customers.

This operated in the same respect that the syndicate operates with prostitution rings today. Whenever one of the girls grew old in one of the houses, saloons or cathouses, she would be replaced.

When the girls got their pay, they had an interest in seeing the town on their days off. Some men didn't want to be seen with a chippie in public but enjoyed them in secret. Therefore, some guys became company keepers to the chippies and whores. The company keepers were paid well and had plenty of sex and fun while giving the saloon girls a night on the town—they were soon labeled gigolos.

The pimps and procurers had not surfaced as yet—they were to come later. All blacks who weren't in slavery were in Africa. Black prostitution was not heard of until after the freeing of the slaves. That is why this is the only guideline that you can find on mackmen, gigolos, pimps and procurers—they are not mentioned in the Holy Bible, textbooks, or libraries. There was no need for black prostitution; the slave masters owned it all. Black sex was at the master's disposal and was as common as drinking a glass of water. But during the exploitation of black women, the white masters discovered something very unusual about the black woman. It was felt that her body's temperature was much warmer. Her vagina was much closer, the velvety skin, plus being blessed with natural grace and rhythm and the movements of her body, made sex much, much more enjoyable. The news quickly spread.

After the freeing of the slaves, black prostitution really began to flourish. It was sometime later, that God decided to create a mate for the black prostitute. To the slave masters, ex-slave men had never been considered as much. When they were first freed they were labeled as wimps. As the years progressed, the black man and woman progressed too. When the white men noticed the administrative ability of blacks, their label was changed from wimp to pimp. That is why the pimp game is a black man's creation and the mediator of the game is called a procurer and he is as essential to the pimp, whore and trick, as oars are to a canoe.

BIRTH OF THE MACK-MAN

Mack-men had been around for quite a while, they became popular not too long after prostitution began to flourish. However, they didn't really surface until the "gold-rush" in California. As the prospectors staked out their claims, the saloon girls, ladies of the evening, and daughters of the night gathered their personal belongings and headed west. The gold diggers were busy digging for gold while the mack-men were busy setting up spots for them when they found it.

Seven girls to a house was all that was necessary. They were called cathouses. The mack-men made a tremendous profit from gambling, whiskey and prostitution. It became a booming business and still exists today.

The mack-men began to expand across the nation. It was from saloon to saloon, then from cathouse to cathouse, later from town to town and today it is from coast to coast. Prostitutes were switched around when they got too common in one place; work could easily be found for them in other places.

As a rule, most mack-men had wives and families but there were some that had some of the women who they started out with. Later it became unpopular to have men watching over women. When a girl became too old as a prostitute but still had the experience, she would usually end up being a whorehouse keeper and from there a madam. Prostitution became syndicated and regular. Today when you hear of bigtime prostitution rings, they are usually controlled by mack-men. There are a few white boys pimping, but that is like a white boy shining shoes, because he can reach higher on the hog. The mack-men were first in prostitution then and also now. The pimp is mostly a black man that took what he had to work with and succeeded.

BIRTH OF THE GIGOLO

There were many cowhands and cowboys who could not stake a claim; all they had was their horses, good looks, and ample time. When most of the saloon and cathouse girls would get their pay, none of her customers would want to be seen parading her in public. When she wanted to paint the town, she would buy companionship. It didn't bother the young handsome cowboys because everything was coming free, plus sex, something that he could not afford to buy. Most of them

began to make a living from entertaining prostitutes
on their nights off. They were paid generously by the
prostitutes. Gigoloing also expanded across the nation.

The whites had staked all the claims and they
had all the gold. Guys in the big cities began to get the
drift and started seeking out wealthy women to escort
and were well rewarded. The trend followed into a big
business and the white boys turned it into a million
dollar enterprise. Escort services began to become
popular and spread all over the world.

Rich heiresses, millionaires' daughters and old,
lonely widows, began to seek out escort services, which
sometimes included a one-night stand. Today, gigolos
are still in hot demand. They always have a list waiting
and they consider it a way of life. Unmarried, handsome young men began to come from far and near trying their hand at gigoloing. Some made it, some did
not. Some got married to their clients and went on to
better things in life. Some stayed in it until they got too
old and had to move over for the younger generation.
They must be white, free, handsome and 21 along with
an outstanding personality, charisma, excellent taste in
clothes and entertaining, a good sense of humor, in addition to being a lady's gentleman.

BIRTH OF THE PIMP

The birth of the pimp is spiced with a type of
factual humor that can be appreciated. There have
been several versions of who was the first pimp and
how the pimp originated. First, it was said the lion, the
king of the jungle, who only stays in the den and watches
over the cubs while the lioness goes and hunts for food
was the first pimp. Then there is Gypsy folklore that
the male had complete control of his band of females—

but that was only in the world of the Gypsies. Next, came the King Pharaoh who showered one of his favorite concubines with every luxury imaginable only to find out he had made a mistake by selecting one of the servant girls. After he determined that he had made a big mistake, he exiled the girl but permitted her to take all her wealth, along with her man, who became an instant pimp.

Regardless of who pioneered the game, the word pimp was never pronounced until after the freeing of the slaves. It was said that it all began with a porkchop sandwich during the days of slavery when the old massa would send to the sleeping quarters of the slave girls to pick one for his night of sexual pleasure. Some slave men would rebel if their woman was chosen only to be beaten with the bullwhip and held at bay with drawn rifles.

But there was one ebony-skinned slave that realized that his head was in the lion's mouth and the only way to get some of what the master had was through his woman.

"Baby what do they do to you when they have you over there?" The young slave would ask his woman.

"They make me have sex with them and give me many kind of nice food and drink that I like," she told him.

"Well the next time they choose you, bring me half of everything they give you," he told her.

The next time she was picked, she returned with a pork chop sandwich wrapped in a dish rag between her legs. Thus, the pimp game was born.

There have been heated debates about the difference between mack-men, gigolos, pimps and procurers. Some Blacks insist on being called mack-men or gigolos. True, it all comes under the same heading. Same as the FBI, policemen, detectives, patrolmen, and security guards. But I believe that a donkey would come closer to becoming a race horse than a Black man would come to becoming a successful mack-man or gigolo.

Today some Blacks may have financial status and may tamper in the field but getting international connection is taboo. When a Black gets involved with a rich or wealthy woman he begins to get the impression that he is a gigolo, but he is only a kept man or a gentleman pimp. You can find more about the gentleman pimp in later chapters. It is a very difficult task trying to prove to him that he is only a gentleman pimp.

Blacks brought from Africa as slaves were forced to become resourceful, remain proud, and survive against unheard of odds. Taking the lowest part of the hog and making it smell and taste like the highest cuts was a declaration of the Blackman's resourcefulness. Today "chitlins" are considered a delicacy worldwide.

Society thought it to be degrading to accept money from a female but it became so rewarding that some poor whites began calling themselves pimps. But this was very rare.

BIRTH OF THE PROCURER

The *procurer* came with the pimp and is very essential to all. He is the mediator; makes all the connections; lines up the tricks for the whores. His type of work is usually with the public, either as a shine boy, bellboy, doorman, cab driver, bartender, or runner. Those positions became so profitable for Blacks that some whites were beginning to reach for these positions.

A procurer is often mistaken for a pimp to the ones who don't know the difference. This also makes

The Sweet Science of Sin such a marketable item for use as a guideline into this game.

The procurer who knows his job is paid handsomely. The cab drivers, bell boys, bartenders, and doormen can demand a 60-40 deal, plus a tip from the John. But the runners and shine boys are considered lucky when they get a tip from the prostitutes.

Most procurers know their business as well as their standard customer. Procurers have their guidelines too. They will not deal with a minor and they will not deal with a John they don't know unless he is recommended by another John that is known.

Every so often, greed by the law will slip through and the procurer and the prostitute are arrested and charged with pandering but not too often. A procurer's work is never done if he is a true procurer. After leaving his place of employment, his apartment can serve just as well. Usually he's got a black book on numerous pretty girls and numerous good-spending Johns. His telephone stays busy, looking for more fish to fry. So God, being just, gave the White boy the macking and gigoloing and the Black boy pimping and procuring. But still the world is not satisfied.

A KING STABLE OF 7-8 WOMEN
THE BIGGER THE BAND, THE SWEETER THE MUSIC

CHAPTER 4
PROFILE OF A KING PIMP

What is a **king pimp**? What makes him tick? A king pimp is the leader of his pack and is just the opposite of the layman. He has the ability to bring out the best in the worst kind of woman. He can understand her trials and tribulations, her unwanted pregnancies, her sometimes incestuous background, her loneliness, her desperation etc.. When the average layman would turn and go in the opposite direction. King pimps are distinctive characters with an exceptional natural intellect who possess the ability to deal with the most difficult tasks with the greatest dignity and ease. He knows his job well, and performs it with painstakingly good taste - that's what makes him tick!

THE KING PIMP

God has blessed us all with some form of talent. Some have beautiful voices but don't utilize or pursue the gift; some are born with grace, charm, rhythm (especially Black people) but won't dance. They are unmotivated like the uncultivated beautiful flower that grows in the wilderness that got trampled and just withered away.

It took 40 years for this author to realize what some people never learn in a lifetime. Science has searched but cannot confirm where the human being really comes from (the miracle of birth) or where he is going after life as we know it (the mystery of death). Yet, some people do capitalize on their gift or gifts while others don't know their callings.

I was selected as a king pimp and I knew what I was here for. That's to care for the stoned females -

the scorned women, to watch over wayward girls, give out lucky numbers and tell others what they are best fitted for, if I become intimate enough with them.

TWELVE COMMANDMENTS OF A KING PIMP AND THE INGREDIENTS THAT MAKE HIM KING

1. He must be strong in mind and spirit. The penis is mightier than the sword. He won't be intimidated and plays past the devil's trickery--jails, drugs, alcohol (the devil's urine) lewd and malicious women and the slander that is uttered from another's mouth.

2. He must be able to control at least 7 to 8 females at the same time. One for each day of the week and if he has the Detroit spirit, the 8th one is a lottery girl. She just keeps his lottery intact. He must handle them with cleverness, shrewdness, intelligence and care, but never with an iron fist.

3. He only makes good sense to the ones that makes good sense to him - sparrows don't fly with eagles and a turkey cannot strut with a peacock.

4. He must be able to withstand any type of criticism, realizing that the layman does not understand the ways of the daughters of the night.

5. He never lets a female be equal with him; Equal Rights (ER) are just a fantasy; it will come back to normal pretty soon. Refuse to have oral sex with your woman unless it is your desire. Do not accept "if you do me, I'll do you." She was put on this earth to

serve men. She may enjoy the thrill that comes with oral lovemaking but deep in the back of her mind she losses respect for you.

The only animals you see licking their sex organs are cats and dogs. The female knows that during a month's time, her vagina accepts so much filth that nature forces a cleaning-out period (menstrual cycle).

6. He goes to combat or resorts to violence in self defense to protect himself, his friends, family, women and some personal possessions.

7. He strikes his females only to shock them back to reality. Toss a bottle at her; hit at her with a golf club, break the mirror over her head; but make sure you don't strike her - that is called a king pimps whipping.

8. Since cleanliness is next to Godliness, he must keep his hygiene habits intact. A shower a day will do and he keeps his physical being in the best condition possible.

9. He never skimps with money when it comes to him and his. You owe the best to you and yours. You might have seen many funerals but you have never seen a Brink's truck follow one.

10. He never worries or broods when one woman goes astray. The story of a man's life is a woman coming and one going; they come better the next time around; they only make room for "A Star," the next one is always better.

11. He only expects to keep a woman a term (4 years) unless he is fortunate enough to get re-elected for another term. If she leaves before her term is up,

then she was not ready for a king pimp anyway. Let her dabble with the other 51 pimp types.

12. There are leaders and there are followers - king pimps follow no mortals, only the shining star.

A TRUE STORY OF A KING PIMP

The king pimp is as much a king in his field as the King of England is. There are many differences in a king pimp and the other fifty-one pimps as there are in noon and midnight.

He has no stress or strain concerning whores. What other pimps try so desperately to do, just comes naturally to him and he is as individual as a fingerprint.

In 1951, Alrico Moss, was a king pimp and wore his crown with dignity, charisma, and grace until his brutal murder in 1973 in a gambling casino in Utah.

At 9:00 a.m., Alrico picked up the mouth piece of the intercom that was built into the headboard of his bed and said,

"Judy, get the girls up and prepare some breakfast. I have an early golf date this morning."

He sat on the side of his bed that was built three steps higher than the floor. He stretched, yawned and frantically scratched his head after slipping into his silk black and red robe and slid his feet into his matching slippers. Before making it to the bathroom, he took one blow of cocaine. After a long shower and a shave, he made it to the dining room where the rest of his "family" patiently waited.

"How's my angels?" he said.

"Fine daddy, as long as you are happy," Judy said.

"How's our daddy this morning?" La Wanda

asked.

"I'm cool, real cool," Alrico told them.

"Orange juice or milk, darling?" Chris asked.

"Milk," he answered and the rest agreed. Six girls were already seated around the table and waited until the other two were seated.

"Girls, there is a little heat on the houses in Peoria, Decauter, and even in Rockford (where his first whore was the madam of a first-class house). The feds got an investigation on at present but it won't last long," Alrico told his fold.

"How long do you think it will last daddy?" one of the girls asked.

"Not long, not long at all. In the meantime, we can play the motels, hotels, conventions and Rush Street," he said as he thrust a fork of egg towards his mouth.

"All the houses of pleasure had been closed down for about two weeks and should be cool soon," he told them.

They all listened patiently before nodding in agreement. "You all realize that this is one big happy family; if ones got, all got. You are sisters. Now money is coming in a little slow but the beat goes on - no one monkey stops the show," he told them.

"Sure you are right, baby," they all agreed.

"Daddy, we are tired of you holding on to that stale bankroll. Al, Chris and I were thinking about taking a trip. We haven't taken a sting in two months," said La Wanda,

"Yes , we might break luck," Chris chimed in.

Chris and La Wanda were drag women (confidence girls).

"You see how essential it is to have wives-in-law. If these whores had to depend on waiting on a drag sting, damn they'd starve to death because they think their cunt is too good to sell," Alrico laughed.

Everyone joined in. "Okay daddy, when do we leave?"   "Tonight, and Mable, you are the only one that's keeping your end up," Alrico lectured. "How much did you put your man's number in for yesterday," he asked the numbers girl.

"I did what you told me, I put $30.00 on 514," she told him. "That's a good girl and do the same thing today, baby," he told his numbers girl. "Judy, you call yourself an (expert shot pick-pocket) and knockout drop artist. You and Lou had better get your act together. Helen you and Precious haven't stole anything recently, get me some new pieces; steal something to sell baby, daddy needs cash," he told his two boosters.

"Baby, I tell Helen that but when she sees something that she thinks you'd like, that's what she takes," said Precious.   Venus could do a little of it all but her best thing was hanging paper (check cashing). With La Wanda and Chris gone on a trip to drag, Mable made sure he had $30.00 on 514, so he could have something to look forward to in the evening time. Judy took off to steal and the rest did what they knew to do best - trying to get their man a fresh bankroll.

Alrico had a lucky number - eight because he had eight hobbies: resting, dressing, reading the funnies, counting the monies, golf, craps, getting the honey and going on shopping sprees. He also had eight women. Alrico was envied and despised by some of the yokels, laymen, and squares yet loved by most women. By him being despised by them, few men grudged his opportunity.

It didn't phase him because God had showed him how to make odds even. Alrico owned two El Dorados, one Lincoln, a luxurious van, plenty diamonds, gold, plenty cash, a Hollywood wardrobe - he was a *King Pimp*. As the weeks turned into months, the ban was lifted from the houses of prostitution around the nation, including the one that Alrico's woman owned in Peoria.

Ruby and Lou went back to work. Judy stole $7,000, and three diamond rings from a "knock out & drop victim". Precious; boosted three mink coats worth $6,000 each. La Wanda and Chris called from New York and had stung $3,000 on the drag tip. 514 came out and Mable had $30 on it. The money was coming in and so was the heat - the law.

Alrico decided he had to beat Chicago. He left the mansion to his mother, packed his caravan and headed to Reno, Nevada with his band of angels, as he called them. They settled in Nevada and after a year of playing Reno, Alrico left for Salt Lake City, Utah, where he heard that the pickings were plentiful.

Once settled in Utah, he built an empire consisting of a super hotel and a classy supper club, adjacent to his house of pleasure. It didn't take long before Alrico had become a Mr. Big in Utah.

Eight was his lucky number for sure. He loved to play dice and whenever he went to a dice game, he would always have a bankroll to gain top respect from the old timers. His bankroll most of the time overpowered the yokels which made him a constant winner and he was known to place a huge amount on eight whenever he could. Things went along okay for the first seven or eight years. He would slip in and out of Chicago to visit his mother and some of his close friends, and sometimes he tried to persuade them to move to Utah.

In the eighth year, things changed. He didn't seem to be able to get close enough to some of the jealous farmers. They started disliking him for some odd reason. He'd always returned them the favors they asked of him. Women all gave him special attention because of his unique charisma. He would, as a rule, avoid trouble by using diplomacy. When he met one of the town's top beauties, a local beauty queen, and she fell madly in love with him, that was the straw that broke the camel's back.

The beauty queen had previously belonged to another Mr. Big. Lola, the beauty queen was born in Salt Lake City, she was a nurse and engaged to Mr. Big until she met Alrico. Alrico and Lola were seen downtown having supper in one of the exclusive supper clubs. Shortly after being seen, Alrico experienced all kinds of traps and pitfalls. His days were virtually numbered.

One afternoon while at home with his angels, Alrico came out of his bedroom and placed a dixie cup at one end of his living room, took his number nine iron and a golf ball and started to practice his putting. Testing his putting skills, he tapped the ball seven times. The eighth time it went in

"Wow, it took me eight tries before I made it; I told you eight was my lucky number," he cheerfully told his girls as they sat on the circular sofa watching him practice.

"I have lived a full life. I will be 58 years old my next birthday and thanks to my angels, I have truly enjoyed life. I'm going out tonight and watch me win. I feel real lucky," he spoke softly to his flock.

He hit the ball again and it went straight into the cup. "See, right in there," he praised himself. He was wearing a white terry cloth robe and black slippers and was quite a handsome fellow. His women just marveled over the texture of his glistening copper-colored complexion.

"Ruby, I almost forgot to mention, you left some wrinkled money on the dresser this morning; next time, take the iron and press it out before leaving it for me," he joked. It brought lots of laughs from his girls.

The girls all took their posts. Alrico showered, shaved, dressed and took $3,000 out of his wall safe for his pocket money and went to the casino. He won big that night but as he was about to make his exit, a big husky guy grabbed both his arms from behind and another one took a ham knife from his belt and repeatedly stabbed Alrico to death.

The killers were apprehended but later freed. The killing of that **King Pimp** will always remain a mystery. Of course, there were rumors that one of Alrico's home angels had a hand in his death. I am afraid we will never know what or who was behind his untimely death.

STACY WITH A FAST-STEPPING WHORE

CHAPTER 5
THE HUMAN BITCH

Webster's Ninth New Collegiate Dictionary defines the word *"bitch"* in several terms, some are: a lewd or immoral woman; a malicious, spiteful and domineering woman; a female dog.

A loose malicious woman is like a loose malicious dog and both are defined as a bitch. The loose dog will mate with as many dogs as she comes in contact with; as many as eight to ten. She is an easy prey for all, and free. After the nights and days of adventure are over, she doesn't make it home with a crust of bread or even a bone. She usually has a belly full of puppies and doesn't know who the daddy is.

When a loose woman commits the same act, she is considered a human bitch. There is as great a difference between a whore, a prostitute and a human bitch as there is morning, noon and midnight. The prostitute is secretive and typically gets her money with a taste of class. The whore is lewd, cunning, sneaky and gets her money anyway she can. But the **human bitch** gets nothing but pregnancy and most of the time doesn't know who the father is.

It is incredible what a fifth of whiskey, wine or drugs can make some loose women do. For some loose women it does not take anything but the opportunity and a willing partner. In any race, the human bitch doesn't consider security, marriage, or any money as important factors - just sex. She gets nothing.

A pimp is supposed to be able to bring the best out, in the worst of women. But to get the human bitch to see the light is a very difficult task, even for him. Society is programmed to the point that if a woman *"gets paid to be laid"* she is a prostitute. That is where their story ends. If she is not going to get security, money or marriage, what is the advantage? If she gets nothing she is considered a human bitch - even by the ones she does it with. When he has had enough, he will inform her *"that she is nothing but a bitch."*

Being criticized by society should be ones least worry, as far as getting *"pay for play"*, because prostitution has a thousand faces. Ask any member of society if they would marry a man if he didn't have a job, was well-off financially or had some other form of security? Could love be a substitute? If *no* is the answer, that is just one of the faces of coated prostitution.

All human bitches have sex for free and consider it just a little sport, not realizing that she is sporting with fire and is subject to get burnt. She sincerely thinks that she is playing a neat little trick on her husband or boyfriend and no one will ever know. But there are three who will always know about it - she knows, her sexual partner knows, and God knows.

Marriage or money doesn't cross her mind because the layman has told her he loves her and he's going to marry her. If she asks for money, then she is a whore and he certainly doesn't want a whore for a wife. There are some areas in the United States that <u>predicate</u> that if you don't get money for sex services, you are considered as something lower than a serpent's belly. Life has its twists and turns, as in the days of Mary Magdalene, Jezebel and Hagar the Harlot, when women were stoned because they accepted gifts for sex. Today, in many areas, you are<u> stoned</u> if you don't.

A whore or a prostitute would not dare spend the night out and come home empty-handed. In the pimp world, a woman who lies with a man for free is scorned. Not only is that a broken code, it affects the prostitution business. For a whore to under-sell another whore is a definite "no-no." A woman's vagina is not like a sandwich. There are no alleys or in-betweens. She either sells it or gives it away (a whore or a bitch). Although there are exceptions to every rule, the average marriage is only a form of prostitution. *"That's my husband or that's my boyfriend."* When you add it all up, the answer is always the same. The husbands have to pay the wives and the tricks have to pay the whores or prostitutes. Only the human bitch is lost in the shuffle.

The woman who commits adultery is a *"daughter of the night."* The woman who accepts money is a whore or a prostitute. The woman who has sex for free is a human bitch. The woman who waited until she was married to engage in sex has not committed adultery and is the perfect specimen of womanhood.

While flying back from California, I engaged in a conversation with one of the pretty stewardesses as she flashed one of the most enchanting smiles that I had ever seen. I kept ordering my favorite drinks just to have an opportunity to chat with her. She was going to lay over in Chicago for a day and a night. I offered to take her to dinner after we had talked about the different types of Chinese foods she liked most. She agreed to meet me in Chicago's China Town at a designated restaurant later that evening.

We met and while eating and sipping cocktails, the subject of sex was broached. She was a very attractive, dark-haired girl of Italian ancestry, the kind that would be hard for any man to resist. After a few more cocktails, she wanted to see some of Chicago's night life. I took her out on the town and made sure she enjoyed herself. It was getting late and I asked her if she had to get back soon. To my surprise, she suggested we "spend some time together." We checked into a small but well-kept South Side hotel.

The next morning, she didn't have to rush back. As a matter of fact she didn't want to return saying,

"Come on Bilbo, let's make love again. I don't have to be back until 5:00 p.m."

"Baby, you are a hotbox. Do you know what you have just given away?" I asked her.

"What?" She asked as she raised up in bed.

"A million dollars worth of love." I told her.

"What do you mean?" she quizzed.

"Baby, you could make a lot of money if you stop giving this heaven away and start selling it. Pretty as you are, you could make a mint," I told her.

"Oh, no! I would never, never do a thing like that. I have had sex with a lot of men from different countries and to have a little roll in the hay if the guy is nice is no big deal. I have given away a lot but I never and would not dare sell my body," she explained wide-eyed.

I said to myself, "Well I'll be damned, *here is a million dollar, beautiful Human Bitch.*"

CHAPTER 6
FIVE OF THE MOST SHREWD FEMALES

Many times the discussion has come up that every woman who associates with a pimp is a prostitute. That is totally false. A wife can make a pimp out of her husband. A mother can make a pimp out of her son. A sister can make a pimp out of her brother. The situation is like putty. You can twist it and turn it any way you desire but when you are finish, it will still be putty.

There are women today who are pimping the "hypocrite pimp"-business women, women of affluent status or well-off financially, working women and wives of other men. It would be difficult to detect because the average woman of today tries desperately to stay out of the grasp of the known pimp but she is the easiest prey on earth for the *"hypocrite pimp."*

Society believes that if a woman associates or affiliates with a known pimp she is a prostitute. There are many women who help men financially but do not want that fact known. Society feels that a "real man" gets on his feet by pulling up his own boot straps, so to speak, and only pimps accept financial favors from a female.

The following are descriptions or definitions of five of the shrewdest females of the shady lane who are tutored by pimps. **Paper-hangers** (forgery and bad check passers), **confidence games** (the pigeon drop or drag), **pickpockets** (shots), **boosters** (thieves that procure brand-new items, right off the racks of the most expensive department stores; such as, fur coats, jewelry, etc.) and the **mother pimps**. These five women

definitely get enough money to support their men ad-
equately, pay off their attorneys or jail fines and still
live comfortably. By no means are they prostitutes. But
like the old adage goes, "all women are potential prostitutes if the money, time or place presents itself."

THE DRAG WOMEN (CONFIDENCE GAME)

"Sonny," the young prostitute spoke, "I've been
peddling my body since I was 18 years old and now I'm
28. I'm tired of some of the things that I have had to go
through. Dealing with those maniacs, drunks, and rapists. Some of them are so unclean. I think I have just
about had my share; I'm just shot." Lucretia said.

"I've been thinking about the same thing- You
are getting too old to be on the fast track" Sonny said
as he sat on the side of the bed where he rested, counting his night's trap.

Lucretia was a tall, very good looking Black
woman who had been a *"daughter of the night"* since
she was a teenager. She had been with many different
men and had just about paid her dues as far as prostitution goes. She had supported several pimps and
whore-houses in her short life span. The time had
come when her mind and thoughts had reached a stage
of maturity and she wanted to make a change.

"I was thinking, I love you Sonny and I love the
game because the game is my life. But I'm getting too
old for this game. Those young whores are walking all
over me," Lucretia stated.

"Well baby, life is elevation. So I'm sure the game
is too. I realize that you are not familiar with the different facets of the game but the *drag* is about your speed.
I know you would rather talk for the money than to lay
down first, getting up last for it, now wouldn't you baby?
Plus, the profits are more plentiful," Sonny told her.

"What is drag?" Lucretia asked coyly.

"Baby, drag is an old confidence game. It's an old game but it's brand new to everyone that hears it for the first time" Sonny told her.

"How does it go?" She quizzed him. "It's a long story baby. "A long story," he said as he put his nights earnings in his robe pocket.

"I'd like to learn how it goes. At least I wouldn't have to tolerate those tricks anymore. What's the penalty for dragging?" She wanted to know.

"In most cases, you beat it because the judge takes into consideration the fact that if the victim didn't have larceny on their minds themselves, they would never have gotten beat (trying to get something for nothing)," Sonny schooled her.

"When are you going to show me how it's done?" She asked him.

"Well, I have a friend called Sly who is a fake (a con-man) and all his women are fakes. I'll get in touch with him and ask him and his women to help you get turned out for me because he and his people are deep into it. But there is a fee for "hipping" you to the game. People just don't give away a million dollar fame for free. He and I are pretty close and I think he'll give me a break."

Within the next two weeks, Sonny got in touch with Sly by telephone and informed him that there was something he wanted to discuss and made a date for the following Friday. They met at a South-side lounge, one of Chicago's finest.

While having their cocktails, Sly said, "You know Sonny, you have been my main man for many, many years and we both have stood on our own two feet but if there is ever something that I can do for you pertaining to a favor, don't hesitate to ask."

"Well that's just what I need now, a favor. You see Sly, this broad of mine is squawking about being too old to hit the fast tracks any longer and she heard about the **"drag"** game and wants to get turned on. What about getting one of your girls to turn her own?"

Sly widened his eyes in amazement. "You mean you want me to hip her to the drag game?"

"Yes."

"Man I thought you wanted to borrow a piece of money." Sly's voice lowered. "Man that will be a difficult job to do. Getting one of these old broads of mine to hip her. They're saying it's too many half-cocked broads out there now. Taking little money and making it bad for the money-getters. I'm too impatient to turn out any more broads but I'll tell you what I'll do, like I did when I first got into it. Talk to old man Smithy. Tell him you are a friend of mine, but he's gonna charge you a nice fee," Sly told him.

"What do you call a nice fee?"

"About $5,000. But she will be ready and will know what she's doing when he turns her loose."

Sly took out his pen and pad and gave Sonny Old Man Smithy's telephone number. Smithy was considered to be a professor in the con game.

The following day Sonny called and finally made the deal. He gave the old man $300 down as good-faith money, and promised him the balance in installments when Lucretia made her first sting. Smithy's tutors were to spend two weeks with Lucretia, teaching her the ropes.

When the time came for Lucretia to hit the stroll for the first time, instead of her having what the con families call beginner's luck (good), she had beginner's bad luck. Sonny went with her and the other two girls on her first day. Lucretia was trained first to play the lost and found game. The two girls walked into Goldblatt's Department Store after following a victim from a nearby loan office. Sonny stood at a distance, serving as a lookout man. The "bunko squad" was all over the store watching for thieves, con artists and pickpockets.

Lucretia approached her first live victim..."Pardon me ma'am, but could you tell me where the lost and found department is? You see, it's not me that wants to know but my girlfriend here. She just found a wallet in that telephone booth with $106 in it. She tried to catch the man outside but he got in a car with out-of-state plates and drove off. She wants to have it advertised, thinking she might get a reward but I think, *she got her reward right now*," she said in a low voice, seeking larceny from the victim.

Then she heard the clicking of Sonny's tongue "click, click, click," indicating to her to freeze the victim; that she had been spotted by the bunko squad. She turned and looked in his direction, he brushed the top of one hand with the other, meaning for her to get out of there; the detectives were heading her way.

Smithy's girl got away but Lucretia, being inexperienced, hesitated, forgetting her sign language and was busted. All of them could have gotten away but when Sonny tried to snatch her he was also busted. They were released on a $1,000 bond for attempt. The victim didn't know what was going on. She was only asked at the trial *"What did the two women say to you?"*

Lucretia learned a dear lesson that she would never forget in life - always pay attention to your accomplice. Remember the signals and signs down to a tee and never forget them.

The next time they took a "vic" for $10,000; $5,000 a piece. They paid Smithy his fee and soon took another $10,000. After that there was no looking back for Lucretia. She took sting after sting.

Her name fell amongst the finest players. When she knocked an old lady off for $50,000, playing the salt and pepper game (Black and White girl team), Lucretia became the most notorious drag broad in the country and she capitalized on telling the biggest lie in the world and became the old "Masterpiece." The **drag pimp** is still around.

PAPER-HANGING (FORGERY)

Bobby Sewell was a genius when it came to imi-
tating someone else's handwriting. The peculiarity of
Bobby's genius was that he was a functioning illiterate.
But he was considered a master when it came to han-
dling fake checks and bank accounts. At any given time,
you could spot Bobby with his thick-rimmed glasses and
attache case, dressed neatly and driving his late-model
powder blue Cadillac El Dorado. Bobby paid all tabs
when eating or drinking with his friends. But none
could pin-point how Bobby maintained his extravagant
lifestyle, which was a mystery to them all. If he was
asked what he did for a living, his reply would be - *I'm
the man that wasn't there."* That was the only answer
one could get from Bobby. Some thought Bobby to be
involved in drugs; some thought he was a jewel thief;
while others thought he was a city employee. But none
thought him to be a paper-hanging pimp.

No one is perfect and neither was Bobby, although he was a master at his trade. He could skillfully
do more with a fake check than a monkey could with a
banana. His first flaw was giving his woman only a small
amount of the money that she went before the gun to
get. His women were the ones who would give the
checks to the bank tellers and yet, they didn't get a fair
cut. Most women would leave Bobby after the first job
was completed because of his stinginess. Bobby was
hardly ever seen with the same female for any length
of time. His money always left him as fast as he earned
it.

His second flaw was being attracted to very good-
looking women. After a big sting, he'd always find himself a very fine female and disappear until he had spent
that bundle and setup things for another bundle.

The people he helped when he was loaded could

care less about him. So it was just a matter of time before Bobby fell on hard times. He had bought a new El Dorado and a home in his new girlfriend's name. After a few weeks of quarreling between the two, she ended up taking the car and home from Bobby. Bobby was at the bottom of the barrel and really didn't have any place to live. His contact where he had his checks printed had refused to cut anymore checks for him until he had paid for the last batch. Bobby's apartment had been broken into and all his check apparatus had been stolen. He drifted back to his roots, the ghetto, where a long-time friend, Harold, had a spare room and made Bobby welcome to whatever he had to offer. After three months, Bobby made a new connection - he found a new printer.

Bobby made arrangements to get all his working tools with one exception, a female to work with him. It didn't take long for him to find a girl, Anna, to go for his line; he told Anna he would make her rich in little or no time provided she listened to him. She agreed. Bobby taught her the ropes from head to toe and she learned well.

One day Bobby told Harold, "Man, I've been eating your food, sleeping in your bed, and using your pad as if it was my own for three months; when I get back, I'm going to repay you for everything. I'm going to bring you so much money that you won't have any place to put it."

"Bobby, you are my friend, man. What I did for you, I believe you would do the same for me. You don't owe me nothing," Harold told him.

Although he knew that Bobby was a big money getter, Harold didn't know how he got his money. Bobby borrowed enough money from Harold to pay the printer for two hundred blank checks and the other necessary items for his trade.

The next morning, Bobby left very early. When

he came back, Anna and another man was with him. Bobby went to the kitchen table while the others stood at attention, watching a genius at work. He made out the checks, all with different amounts. Next he certified them and matched the handwriting from the original checking account that he had borrowed from the other man with him. After his completion of the two hundred checks, all three left. That was the first time Harold had any knowledge where Bobby had been getting so much money over the years.

It was 9:00 a.m. when they left. Around 8:00 p.m., Bobby, Anna and the friend pulled up in a brand new Pontiac loaded with groceries and several packages of meat. They all grabbed shopping bags and headed upstairs. Bobby held on to one shopping bag, telling Harold to come with him while Anna and the other man helped bring the groceries upstairs. Bobby emptied the shopping bag on the living room carpet and large bills came tumbling out.

"Harold, help me count this money and when you count up to a thousand, put a rubber band around it."

When the other man and Anna came in the room, Bobby gave the man a thousand dollars and told him thanks. The guy left, telling Bobby that anytime he needed him in the future, just give him a call.

Anna sat down on the floor with Bobby and Harold and helped to count the money. When they had finished counting, there was nearly $8,000. Bobby gave Harold $1,500 and told him he would catch him later. After Bobby and Anna left, Harold stood at the window wondering, *"Where in the world did he get that much money in one day?"*

Bobby continued with his new star Anna and soon bought himself another powder blue Cadillac and gave the Pontiac to Anna to work in.

Not long afterwards, Bobby's Anna became friends with a girl who worked in a bank. When she explained to Bobby where the girl worked, Bobby's genius mind started spinning.

"Can she listen?" Bobby inquired.

"She said she would. I screened her good and she really needs some money," she told him.

"Well bring her by for dinner Sunday, I want to talk with her."

That Sunday, Anna picked up the girl from the bank and they went shopping. When they came back, Anna introduced Bobby to the girl.

"Bobby, this is Edna, Edna this is Bobby, my sweetie."

"Hi baby, sit down. I really want to talk to you. Go fix us a drink Anna."

Anna went to the bar to get the drinks.

"How do you like yours Edna?" She called from across the room.

"On the rocks," Edna replied.

"Anna tells me you work at Gateway Bank, are you a teller?" Bobby asked.

"No, I work in the collateral department."

"That's even better" he said.

"Well, how is it that that is better, I can't cash any checks? I don't even come close to any money."

"Listen baby, in the collateral department, just bring out a bank book belonging to a woman patron, making sure there is enough in the account so that it can be worth our while. We'll use it one day and you place it back the next. You understand where I'm coming from?" he asked her.

"You mean all I have to do is steal a bank book and use it for one day and then put it back the next?"

"That's all you've got to do. Anna and I will handle the rest." They agreed.

The next day Edna brought Bobby a bank book with $18,000 in it. Bobby wrote out a withdrawal slip for $9,000 and gave it to Anna.

"Now baby, all you have to do is pass this slip to the teller with the withdrawal slip inside. She'll just ask you how do you want it and tell her in big bills," Bobby schooled her.

Just like clockwork, Anna walked in the bank, passed the book to the teller. "How do you want it?" the teller asked.

"In big bills please," Anna replied. The teller counted out $9,000. The signature on the withdrawal slip matched the signature on the bank's signature card perfectly.

Bobby gave Edna one-third of the take, leaving him with $6,000. Edna was very pleased. Now the wheels really began to turn. Bobby, Edna and Anna were taking money so fast and abundantly it looked like Ft. Knox. Bobby and Anna moved to a beautiful home in an exclusive section of Chicago's South-side called Pill Hill and Edna moved in with them. For the next two years, Bobby lived in luxury. Staying at home and sending Anna and Edna out, occasionally using a new face. After two more years, they moved to New York. Edna went along. Chicago never heard of Bobby Sewell again but the forgery pimp is still around.

THE PICKPOCKET

Pick-pockets come in many phases. Cutting pockets or purses of passengers on public transportation or going in an old lady's bag stealing her wallet, doesn't make one a glamorized thief in the eyes of the so-called experts of the *"larceny from the person game."*

They are looked upon as the lower-class of thieves. The phases accelerate categorically as thief, shot, whiz and cannon. When you reach the stage of cannon, you have reached the epitome, a real champion pick-pocket! To become a cannon, one must put in many, many long hours because he is the best and come no better. That's what Bubble Morris was, *a king in his field.*

As early as 10 years old, Robert Morris had a natural talent for stealing money from his father's pockets as he slept. At times, his father would awaken, and catch Robert in his room and Robert will tell him that he just came in the room to see how he was doing, with one hand still in his father's trouser pocket. As the years passed, Robert graduated from a bed-post thief to a street thief. He learned different techniques from older professionals to become a master of the art. Step by step, he moved up higher and higher - from a pocket thief to a whiz. Then he gained the status as a *"shot"* and later was labeled a *"cannon"* the pinnacle of the pickpocket game.

He was nicknamed "Bubble" because he was always chewing bubble gum while he worked. He was caught once at an airport stealing $15,000 cash from an inside coat pocket. When the police searched him, they found the loot and 10 packages of bubble gum. That labeled him the *"Bubble Gum Kid."* He was only 19 years old at the time. The name stuck and he had been called Bubble Morris ever since, until his death in 1946.

Bubble went from state to state and played each big city's airports, carnivals and race tracks. At all major sporting events, you could always find Bubble and his mob plying their trade. He was considered, not only by his associates but by the Bunko Squad as well, the *"King of the Cannons."*

Bubble Morris could perform miracles when it came to stealing money from a person's pocket while standing, talking to them. He once stole $100 worth of coins from a man's overalls while standing next to him at a dice table without ever being suspected. He could talk to a person, placing one hand on his shoulder while using the other hand to lift his wallet (hide). The experts still consider these as almost impossible feats.

In order to become a *"cannon,"* one must be able to perform unbelievable feats. All of the women and men of the shady lane were awe-struck by and admired Bubble Morris's flamboyant lifestyle and his reputation of always keeping large bankrolls, to say nothing of his generosity. Whenever Bubble Morris left any major event many, many wallets left with him. But as the years took its toll as in many professions, Bubble's skills began to wane, as recognized by the Bunko Squad detail. Bubble had to come up with another gimmick.

The idea he came up with made him the *"pickpocket pimp."* He started a school for the women that loved, admired and adored him. He taught them the basics or fundamentals, in detail, on how the game was really executed.

Of course, a large segment of our American society could care less about individuals in the shady lane life but Bubble Morris is still discussed in the same respect as some major league ball players in NFL hall of fame.

Because of poor eyesight and waning skills, Bubble had to move to the back burner. But, Jen took over where her man left off. Jen, who was Bubble Morris' main woman, gave Bubble a few pointers on how to become a cannon - some say those were only rumors. Jen had so many scars in her face it looked like the spiraling veins of a road map - but she was a CANNON.

In spite of the scars, her face was new to the police and to victims. In one year at the Kentucky Derby, Jen was caught with her hand in a senator's pocket. He yelled for help, the police arrived, and caught Jen as she tried to flee. She was arrested and taken to jail. She didn't have enough money to post her bond of $2,000. Being in a small branch of jail she was refused use of the telephone. She patiently waited until the shift changed. At 2:00 a.m. she called out for the old fat turnkey. Using her femininity in a very tempting manner, she took off her panties and stretched out on the cold, steel bunk in a cat-like pose. She had to call out to him twice, before he finally answered.

"Yeah, what you want?" he bellowed. She asked him to come back to her cell to determine the problem.

Jen was practically nude, still in that inviting pose, exposing just the parts of her body that she knew would turn him on. She had scars on her face but had a body that was like smooth brown satin. The turnkey's sexual desires quickly awakened.

"Whatcha want girl?" He hollered in a southern drawl while his eyes drifted over her lovely brown body.

"Would you do me a favor?" Jen sensuously asked as she sat up on the bunk, widening her legs and exposing her vagina and hoping he asked for a sexual favor in return.

The plan worked perfectly. As he asked, "If I do something for you, whatcha you gonna do for me?" He grinned looking at her with great lust.

"I just want a blanket, it's so cold in here," she said.

"I don't mind doing you a favor, but one favor deserves another," he said, trying to get his point across.

"Anything you want big man," she purred.

It was 3:30 a.m. Knowing that no one was around, but a couple of drunks sleeping it off on the other side of the jail, he rushed to the store room and got two blankets and a pillow. He rushed back, nervously unlocked the cell, hurriedly pulling his pants down to have sex with her however, in his excitement, he lost his erection.

"Here, let me help you," and she began to give him oral sex, rubbing and squeezing him tightly while her educated fingers lifted his wallet, removing six $100 bills and two $20 bills; she replaced the wallet in his pocket while he was in a sexual frenzy. After the sex session was over, he smiled like a Cheshire cat.

"Would you be so kind as to fix me a cup of coffee and a sandwich?" She cajoled him as she watched every move he made with the keys.

"Sure honey, anything for you."

He rushed to the small space that served as a kitchen, not bothering to lock her jail cell. She noticed, that he had put the car keys to his old personal car in the desk drawer just outside the cell. He came back to her with a thick sandwich and said that the coffee was still brewing. He left to check on the coffee and laid the jail-house keys on the desk with the keys to the outer doors on that key ring. Jen slowly and quietly tiptoed over to the desk, got the keys, unlocked the outer doors and escaped in the turnkey's old personal car. When he came back with the steaming coffee, she was long gone. She abandoned his car at the first truck stop she came to and hitched a ride to a bus depot in the next town. She made it back to Chicago safely with $600 more than what she had hidden in her wig.

That's just one of the many feats that a CANNON can perform! The pickpocket pimp is still around.

THE BOOSTER

As the pimps, prostitutes, boosters, hustlers and whores gathered around the long circular bar enjoying their cocktails, anxiously trying to out-spend the other, in walked Big Lou, queen of the boosters. Her voice could be heard all over the place as some of the men got up to give her their seats.

"Yeah, all you flat-backs, chili pimps, pussy selling poor bitches, get back from the bar, Big Lou is here. One of my day's work is equivalent to one of you whore's week's work," she bellowed.

"You couldn't be talking to me honey because

I'm a thief and a damn good one," said the pretty young upcoming booster.

"The type of stealing you do, small time bitch, could never rate with me. See bitch, you might make two or three hundred dollars a day, taking that cheap shit, cloth coats, dresses, pants-suits, skirts and slacks. But me, I wouldn't come home without a thousand or more. I steals hair (fur) and as far as that little punk-ass-nigger you got over there, I wouldn't have him to shine my mother-fucking shoes. See, I'm a woman and I've got to have a man, even if I have to make a man out of him myself. I'm a queen bitch and I'll make me a king. I'm a grand theft bitch. Give these poor ass bitches a drink," she said as she pulled up a huge bank-roll of $50 and $100 bills.

"You must want my man cause nobody else even mentioned him but you, Miss Big Lou! And another thing, I don't want your drink. I'm not thirsty," shouted the pretty young thing.

"Bitch, you look like you thirsty to me," said Big Lou.

"Well I'm not and I don't give a damn how much money you make a day cause as big, Black and ugly as you are wouldn't no decent man be seen in public with you - with your gorilla-looking ass." "Since I've just got to be your bitch, at least I'm a *young, pretty bitch*. I don't need money to have a man," the young pretty girl said.

The rest of the patrons looked on, some grinning outwardly and some grinning under their skin. Two old-time pimps turned and left the lounge. Big Lou and the young girl continued their argument.

"That big Black bitch, Lou, didn't lie about the kind of money she makes. She keeps a brand new Cadillac every year and one for her man and she's been doing it for years," cited the first man.

"Now that's the type of woman I wouldn't mind

having" said the second man.

"She's not going to deal with you. You're too old for her, she likes them real young so she can raise them to her hand," the first man said.

"The other young whore is a pretty bitch," said the second man.

"Yeah, she's pretty but she's not one-third as pretty as those hundred dollar bills Big Lou's got," the first man gleamed. They both shook hands and broke out in a big laugh. "But she's crazy about those young punks and she's extremely generous to them -from Cadillacs on down. She molds them into whatever she wants them to be," the last one said.

About two weeks later, the headlines of the Black Dispatcher (Chicago Defender) read:

*"**THE QUEEN OF THE BOOSTERS WAS AR-RESTED IN MILWAUKEE IN LORRE'S FUR SHOP. SHE WAS CAUGHT WITH TWO, FULL LENGTH MINK COATS, A CHINCHILLA AND A SILVER FOX VALUED AT OVER $65,000.**"*

In the same lounge, Big Lou was the topic of conversation. "Now that, that big, Black, gorilla-look-ing bitch is preparing to take a vacation, maybe a young pretty bitch can have a chance," said the same young thief that was arguing with Big Lou two weeks previously.

Big Lou was sentenced to four years in Dwight Correctional Center for Women but that was just a step for a stepper and Big Lou was a stepper. She had been there many times.

The oddest thing about Big Lou was whenever she got busted, she would always have her cars left in a garage until she was released so that her young man would not be driving any young, pretty whores around in either one of her cars.

When her four years were up, Big Lou came home and all she could hear was Margo this and Margo that.

"Who in the hell is Margo?" she asked.

After she had hit the streets, they gave her a big party. Margo came too; the same young girl Big Lou had tried to belittle before she was sent up.

Now that Margo had taken over the hair game (furs), she and her man had made it to the pinnacle of the thief game. She drove up in a brand new Lincoln and dressed all in mink, her man was wearing a full-length mink too. She sent champagne over to Lou but she refused it.

"I just want to say one thing Miss Big Lou, I'm glad to see you home. I learned a lot from you but you have had your day; your case is closed; you have lost your reflexes. Your eyesight is failing and so is your coordination, agility and your balance. It's time for the young to perform. Why don't you retire? You've spent half of your life in and out of the joint, you are through," Margo said.

"Retire my ass, bitch. You couldn't rate with me if I was 100 years old," Big Lou said. They talked a while and Margo got up to leave.

"*Bye old bitch*," she said as she left out of the door. The music was loud but the laughter drowned out the melody as the party went on.

A month later Margo and another booster took a trip to Alaska. The word had gotten around that minks of all kind were hanging on the outside of stores in Alaska, they were plentiful and considered easy picking. They took a few mink jackets, stone-martins and stoles and sent them back to their men. But fate stepped in. They got busted with four full-length minks in their car, as the coats were identified by the tags they bore. They were sentenced to five years each in a women's Alaskan reformatory.

No one has heard of either Big Lou or Margo for quite a while. Some say they are still around; some say Margo completed her sentence and upon her release, became a top dope peddler. The booster's pimp is still around.

THE MOTHER PIMP

Angela Wade was a rare specimen of a female. Even before she was born, it was often remarked that if the baby inherited its parents features it would be a wonder to admire. Angela's mother was an octoroon (a Black with one quarter Black blood) and her father was of Italian heritage, the mixture making them both attractive people.

At the age of 15, Angela could have easily been mistaken for 18, because of her stature and feminine endowments. Her beauty was of such that she was openly admired by both boys and men and envied by the women. Angela's mother's beauty came close to having the same mesmerizing effect upon men when she was a younger woman. But in Roberta Wade's young life, men taught her a lesson that she would never forget; they taught her the mean side of life.

Roberta had been a dance-hall girl, prostitute, and you name it. She had been beaten and dragged to the lowest ebb of life. She survived it all but made a vow to herself that her daughter would never endure in life what she had undergone. After her husband walked off, when Angela was a small child, Roberta, uneducated, broke and because of the hard street life, had lost most of her good looks. She was somehow able to piece her life back together, she applied for welfare and quit the street game to raise her daughter.

From a very small child Angela was taught that men were dogs, no good, never to be trusted, and to use them strictly for profit. On this subject, Roberta tutored Angela constantly.

Angela attended Hyde Park High School, not far from the eight-flat apartment building where she and her mother lived on Chicago's South-side. Due to Angela's beauty, it was very difficult to keep the boys at bay. Mrs. Wade had done an excellent job of alienating Angela from others, especially men and boys, and Angela didn't believe or listen to anyone except her mother. As a consequence, the flirtations from the men and boys were completely ignored.

Angela had graduated high school and was now 18 years old, 5 feet 6 inches tall, weighed 120 pounds, with hair as black as night that hung down below her derriere, which was usually worn in one braid. The femininity in her walk let everyone know she was all woman and more. But the ladylike manner in which she carried herself told them "hands off."

Whenever Angela went to the store or laundromat, Roberta would see her in the company of George, a young black guy who lived in the neighborhood.

"Why do you always want to be with that little black nappy-head boy?"

Angela replied chuckling, "Oh mummy. George is just a friend. I have a lot of fun with him and he's harmless."

"Well it just don't look right. A lot of people think there is something going on between you two. You can only bring yourself down by rubbing shoulders with certain types of people, you understand?"

"Yes mother," Angela said.

The landlord's son, Rodney, was quite handsome and thought he was every lady's dream man. He expected Angela to chase him as the rest of the dark-skinned girls did. However, his ego was deflated when he and his new automobile went unnoticed by Angela.

He had a new car, his parents owned several apartment buildings around the city, he had his own apartment in one of his parent's buildings, and could not understand her aloofness towards him. But the more she ignored him, the more his desire and determination that she was going to be his woman increased. He would pass Angela on the walkway at times and act as if he didn't notice her. Angela did notice him but he was not her type of man. He was too pretty and looked like a white boy. She liked dark-skinned men.

Angela enrolled in a local junior college and was coming home one day after classes when Rodney's red sport's car stopped in front of her. He was the first to break the hard cake of ice. "Hi neighbor," he said in a flirtatious manner. She turned, looked back and kept stepping without a reply.

At the same time, she saw George and waved out to him. When she got in the house, she put her books down and removed her coat.

"Ma, who's that creep in the red car? He's always hanging around here?" she asked her mother as she pointed out the window.

"Oh, now that may be a good catch for you. He's the landlord's son and manages another building on the Westside for his parents, so I heard," her mother told her.

"He's a creep, he thinks he's hot stuff," Angela said.   "He's just like all men, he'll have you for free if you let him. No marriage, no security, and no money unless you know how to handle them and you should know as long as I have been telling you how to treat a man. If you are not on top there is no deal. Somebody's got to be on top and the only way you can get on top of a man is to use the tools that God gave you to work with. Make him chase you, that's where the thrill is, the thrill is in the chase with a man 'cause honey, once he grunts and groans, the thrill is gone. And child let me tell you, behind that comes a chill and the chill is a bitch," the mother lectured her beautiful daughter.

"I know mother, I know," replied Angela.

"So, you make a man wait as long as you can. Make him spend, get him strung out and let him play catch. As long as you can keep your panties on, you are winning and when you take them off, you've lost. If a man can get what he wants free what's the use of paying for it -you understand child?" She lectured on.

"But mother, isn't that called prostitution?"

"Honey, people are going to call you something either way it goes. You see, if you give away your body, you're just like the other dogs in the street-five male dogs chasing one female dog. After each one has sex, they disappear. The she-dog is called a bitch. She's not going to have a bone when she finally makes it home to her master. And if you get something out of sex dear, you are called a whore. This is the American system so you take your pick child." Her mother scolded her.

Angela looked at her mother and thought to herself, *"some man really did a job on my mother."*

Now, the landlord's son definitely wanted Angela and had made it his business to find out as much about her as he could. He found out from his father that Mrs. Wade attended church every Sunday. One Sunday morning, knowing Angela would be home alone, he got permission from his father to go and ask why the rent was late.

But before he got to her door, he saw her emptying the garbage. "You need help?" he smiled.

"No thank you, I can handle it myself," she said.

She walked back to her door and locked it. Rodney rang the doorbell. She came to the door and just stood there, with her hair hanging loose around her body.

"Yes," she said.

"I was just trying to collect the rent today," he said with a pen and receipt book in his hands.

"Well, you will have to wait until my mother comes from church, she handles those things," she told him.

"You know, I've been noticing you, what's your name?" he asked.

"Angela, Angela Wade," she said, while her beauty engrossed him.

"Mrs. Wade's daughter. Oh yeah", he said. "Do you ever go out?"

"I'm not feeling well, I have a very bad cold," Angela replied.

"Why not take a spin with me sometime and let me show you around?"

"I'm sorry, but I don't go out with men."

"What do you go out with, girls? I sure wish I was a girl. Well, if you change your mind, let me know."

Later that evening, Angela couldn't wait until her mother got home from church to tell her the news. After she told her mother what had happened, her mother said, "That bastard didn't want no rent. Today is just the 31st and we don't pay rent 'til the 1st. I know what he wanted."

"I thought it sounded kinda fishy, he asked to take me out." Angela told her mother.

"Well the next time that he ask you, you accept his invitation. We'll pay his parents rent and you can get it back out of him. Make him take you to a very expensive restaurant, no alcohol but eat heartily; make him spend but don't go to bed. Tell him you will not go to bed with a man until you are married and that you are saving yourself for your husband. Talk marriage to him, that will keep him at bay," her mother coached.

For the next three weeks, whenever they saw each other, it would only be casual hellos. Angela was well trained. But, finally the chase was too great for

Rodney. She had worn down his resistance.

"Angela you act as if you have something against me. Do you?" he asked her one day.

"Of course not, why would you think a thing like that, you are my landlord and I respect you. I've been waiting for an invitation but you stopped asking to take me out?"

His eyes widened. "If I decided to go out with a man, it would be with you," she told him.

"Well, I certainly will be glad when you decide,".

The next day, Rodney was waiting for her when she came out of school. "Can I drop you off Angela?" he asked.

"Well, I don't suppose it would hurt anything," she answered, smiling beautifully to herself, Angela knew she had caught this big fish as visions of dollar bills danced in her head.

Rodney hurriedly opened the door on the passenger side, she hopped in, and he drove off. On the way home, he asked Angela for a date, but she informed him he would have to talk with her mother first and suggested that he come back that same night at 8 o'clock. He agreed and watched her as she dashed up the stairs -she was his dream girl.

At 8 o'clock sharp, Rodney was ringing the Wade's doorbell. Angela answered the door and welcomed him inside. Roberta was thrilled but held herself in check, she knew she had schooled her daughter right. He had the right complexion, hair, and security to boot!

Roberta and Rodney were introduced by Angela and Roberta insisted that he stay for dinner (as if that wasn't her plan all along).

She had prepared a scrumptious dinner with the fancy tablecloth and her best dinnerware. Roberta took over the conversation and in no time flat, she had turned the conversation to marriage. Rodney didn't have too much to say on that subject as marriage was not exactly what he had in mind. But he was enjoying the dinner and being there with Angela.

Roberta pumped Rodney for personal information about his family and got the information she was after. He was an only child and would, of course, eventually inherit everything his parents owned.

Roberta was enraptured in the fact that in the last three weeks, Rodney and Angela had been inseparable. He had taken her to several expensive restaurants downtown, a couple of plays, the movies, and a boat ride on the lake. He was spending money like it was going out of style. All along, Angela had refused any alcoholic beverages although Rodney had tried to persuade her to have a martini or at least a sip of champagne. But she stood her ground, remembering her mother's lectures. He tried his best to get her to accompany him to a hotel but was refused in such a manner that he couldn't get angry or upset.

"Angela, do you know that when a man becomes so emotionally charged up for sex and doesn't do anything about it, it deteriorates his body? Baby I'm burning for you," he told her.

"I know Rodney. I like you well enough to keep your body from deteriorating but I want you for my husband and I'm saving my body for my husband. Is that wrong?" she asked him tenderly.

Rodney had a little money saved and marriage was frightening but what good is money when you can't have the things you want out of life, he thought to himself. After a few more dates, Angela's charm and beauty overwhelmed him and he found himself proposing to her. She said yes and he bought her an exquisite one and a half karat engagement ring. They were married on her 20th birthday.

For the next four years, things seemed to be working out fairly well. Angela had made her mother very, very comfortable, sparing nothing. She dropped out of college when she became pregnant shortly after the marriage and gave birth to two more children in rapid succession. Now they had two girls and a boy. Despite the many household chores brought on by the children, Angela still became bored with her life and decided to start looking for a job. Her mother had agreed to keep the children. She auditioned for a job modeling shoes for an expensive shoe store downtown and got the job with no hitches. Rodney was not exactly happy about the idea but he cared so much for her he wanted to see her happy.

At the job, Angela had proposition after proposition spring up from all directions. Some by male customers and some by co-workers. She began to share with her mother all of the opportunities that were being shoved her way and being married, she was a little in doubt about how to handle the situation.

But her mother solved that problem by telling her, "Girl, you are not going to be young and pretty but once. Your beauty is going to fade away so you had better get it while you can. You don't have to tell your husband all your business because I bet he don't tell you all of his."

Not long after that conversation, Angela accepted a date from a persistent customer who was somewhat of a rich Casanova. As the affair continued, and bloomed Angela was being showered with gifts. Not just trinkets but the real stuff; a diamond bracelet, a sapphire and diamond necklace with matching earrings, and so on.

Her mother knew all about the affair and even applauded it, keeping all the jewelry at her house so Rodney wouldn't discover it. All the cash Angela received, was deposited in the bank in a secret account she had opened for this purpose. Before the affair started, Angela never wanted to go any place without first consulting her husband, but now things were different.

Of course, with all of the rendezvous and sometimes late hours Angela kept, not bothering to tell Rodney when or where she was, suspicions of infidelity started to creep into Rodney's mind. Even their sex life had fallen off. Most of the time, Angela would plead she was tired, had a headache, or I don't want another baby.

Rodney decided to set a trap for her and told her he had to take a business trip to California for a week and made her promise not to go out at all while he was gone and she agreed. Up until this point he had never suspected her of any wrong-doing but he was almost sure something was up.

She helped him pack his bag neatly and when the cab arrived to take him to the airport, she accompanied him to the cab, kissed him good-bye, telling him how much she would miss him. When he arrived at the airport, he called her, told her how much he loved her and that his plane would be leaving in 30 minutes. He gave her a number to call him back in 15 minutes because he had to call the office. After about 12 minutes, the PA system was paging Mr. Rodney Pellow. He answered the page and was informed he had a telephone call.

Angela said sweetly, "you told me to call you back, Rod."

"Yes baby, I just wanted to hear your sweet voice again before I left and to tell you how much I love you." he said, meaning every word.

"I love you too, Rod."

"Well, I'd better get going, passengers are boarding my flight. I'll call you from California tomorrow and I'll see you when I get back. Be sweet."

Rodney immediately hailed a taxi and headed to a local hotel, checked in and remained there for three days. He telephoned Angela every day as though he was calling from California. On the third day, he went to their house while Angela was working and searched the entire place, looking for anything suspicious but didn't find anything.

While he was still in the house, he heard Angela coming in. He hid in the kitchen closet where she would never look. After about a half an hour he heard the telephone ring. He listened as Angela answered the phone.

"Hello, Larry, I'm so glad you called. I thought you were angry with me. My old crazy husband took a trip to California and I just couldn't make it. Do you still love me?" Angela asked the party on the phone.

"Tonight? Yes, he'll be gone for the rest of the week. At 8? Yes, I'll be ready at 8 o'clock sharp. Just park in the front and I'll see you then. I love you, Larry," Angela told the caller as she hung up the phone.

Rodney felt so hurt, humiliated, cheap and furiously and dangerously angry. He tried to think but anger blinded him. He finally cooled down enough to figure out what to do.

He decided to remain there, in the closet, until her date, Larry, came to pick her up and he would surprise both of them. He didn't know what he was going to do but he knew he wanted to tell Larry to leave his wife alone. At about 5 minutes to 8, Angela left the house.

Rodney eased out of the closet, peeped out the window and saw her standing outside, waiting for her date. When Larry drove up and Angela approached the car to get in, Rodney was already down the stairs and he grabbed the car door on the driver's side, screaming and pulling Larry out of the car. He really wasn't conscious of what he was doing, all he could see was red.

Rodney attacked Larry so fast, he didn't have a chance to defend himself. Rodney was really giving it

to him but somehow Larry got away, and ran down the
street with blood running from his face.

Angela was screaming and Rodney turned to her
and started beating her. She ran back upstairs to the
house, he followed and continued to beat her in the
house. Finally, he came to his senses and ran out the
back door. Someone had seen or heard the commotion
and called the police, however, when the police arrived,
Rodney was already gone. Angela lay in a pool of blood
unconscious. It was no beautiful creature laying there,
just a woman covered with blood.

The police rushed her to Billings Hospital Emer-
gency. She had a concussion, two black eyes and re-
quired 52 stitches. Angela remained at the hospital for
four weeks. The officers who took her to the hospital
visited her regularly. One of the officers had fallen for
her deeply. Upon her discharge he was there to take
her to her mother's house.

Roberta went berserk when learning of her
daughter's plight. After finding out that Angela would
live, Roberta was partially relieved and urged her to
get a divorce from Rodney as soon as possible, which
she did.

After the divorce, Rodney moved out of town
and the only time Angela heard from him was when he
sent money for child support. Angela and the children
never returned to their house and the police officer
acted as her personal body guard and new lover. Larry,
apparently was so frightened by the beating both he
and Angela took that he sent someone back to pick up
his car, he wanted no part of Angela anymore.

Although the policeman was married, he was
very generous to the whole family and spent many hours
at their house, watching and guarding Angela, his love.

But that love was short lived. The officer apparently found himself another love. A famous vocalist arrived in town and advertised for a personal body

guard. Angela's boyfriend took the assignment much to Angela's dissatisfaction. The policeman was getting tired of Angela by then and desired the vocalist over Angela anyway. So he strayed away.

From then on, there was no looking back for Angela and Roberta Wade, her mother. It was war against men. Angela would not date a man unless he was rich. She married a young, wealthy minister a short time later, whined him into buying her a mansion and moved her mother and stepfather in with her and the children. With her mother's assistance, she cleaned the minister out and divorced him, getting the mansion in the divorce settlement. He was her first victim.

Her next victim was a White furniture tycoon; a millionaire who fell deeply in love with Angela. She couldn't marry him because he was already married but she did manipulate him and his money enough to put him into Bankruptcy Court.

Next, Angela decided she wanted to go into the cosmetology business. She studied for her license to open shop and in the meantime she met a well-established, prominent attorney who purchased the building where she would house her 22 chair beauty spa. She kept that business for six years remarried a well-known male vocalist who purchased her another mansion. This mansion would have qualified to be shown on TV's "Rich and Famous."

Now, Angela is in her 50's, her children, out of good colleges and well-established on their own. She lives with her mother in her "Rich and Famous" mansion, not the least concerned about men, having divorced her last husband.

"My mother told me not to ever give a man a dime and to get all that I can from those dirty bastards and bring it all home to her and that is just what I did, and will do forever," Angela will tell anyone.

CHAPTER 7
CRIMES THAT PIMPS DO NOT COMMIT

Pimps and prostitutes do live by a code of ethics. Society continues to frown upon these professions but do they ever ponder why most heinous crimes are committed by those not of this lifestyle?

During my lifetime, I've heard some treacherous tales of crimes committed by society, <u>not</u> pimps and prostitutes. Here are a few of those stories:

1. The torso of a 28 year old Chicago school teacher was found in Portage, Indiana two days after the woman allegedly had an argument with her husband, a physician, at his west side office. Shortly after the torso was found, authorities speculated that the victim's body had been dismembered by someone trained in the medical profession which subsequently led to the extensive questioning of the victim's husband.

2. A Cook County Deputy Sheriff was indicted on a charge of murder in the death of his wife who was allegedly shot in the head after an argument over her desire to become a *Jehovah Witness*. The deputy sheriff was charged with murder and armed violence in the October death of his wife who was shot once in the forehead. The officer told authorities he had his weapon cradled and was test firing it when a bullet accidentally discharged, hitting his wife. Reportedly he had emptied the gun earlier. However, investigators said that moments before the shooting, the two were arguing about her desire to leave the *Roman Catholic Church* and become a *Jehovah Witness,* a subject of heated de-

bate for several days.

3. After eight years of alleged beating and tor-
tures, a South-side woman's worst fears were realized
when her former husband, armed with a shotgun and
pistol, reportedly broke into her home and shot her to
death and wounded three family members. The
woman died almost instantly after allegedly being shot
about 10 times at close range when the irate gunman,
opened fire on occupants in the house where the wife
had been living for several days. The gunman, a public aide recipient with a prior arrest record for unlaw-
ful possession of a weapon, reportedly vowed that he would
never be taken alive.

4. Hours after admitting he mutilated a Chicago
prostitute a 25-year old alleged devil worshiper was
found guilty of the woman's 1981 murder. Prosecutors
asked for the death penalty. The killer was already serving a life term with no parole for his part in four other
murders. He had been serving a 120-year sentence for
the attempted rape and murder of another Chicago
prostitute in October 1982. In a cool, calm and collected
tone, he recalled how he and the "cult-leader" picked
up the victim in a van and drove her to a bushy area.
After killing and mutilating her, they both sexually as-
saulted her.

5. A Syracuse psychologist once appeared in
court on a charge of sexual assault against a 9-year old
girl after admitting intimate contact with the child, police said. He was charged with aggravated criminal
assault after a police investigation which started with a
telephone tip. Police found the psychologist, who
claimed to be in Chicago for a medical conference, in
bed with the girl, at a North Michigan Avenue hotel room

with pornographic material in the room. The psychologist told a detective he had been giving the girl sex education, with permission from the mother, a long time friend, who allegedly arranged the meeting. The girl was placed in protective custody until it could be determined whether the mother played any part in the alleged abuse.

Here is a letter that was once sent to advice columnist Ann Landers:

Dear Ann Landers:

Your recent column on father-daughter incest makes me wonder about my own victimless crimes. I am in my early 60's, divorced and retired. My sister is in her late 50's and widowed. We go to bed together twice a week. This has been going on since her husband died eight years ago.

Actually, when we were teenagers, we fooled around a lot but never had intercourse. This is not a love match but it is sex and good sex at that. We both enjoy these escapades and they always produce a good night's sleep. No one knows about this and no one is getting hurt. Do you think we are fooling ourselves?

No Name, No City please.

Dear No Name:
Sick, sick, sick. If I had your address, I would send you a get-well card. You say no one is getting hurt. I disagree. While you and your sister are practicing incest, you are denying yourselves the opportunity to have normal relationships with others. I am talking about marriage. The fact that neither of you see anything wrong with such behavior suggests a moral dead-spot that is unnatural and revolting.

THE LIFESTYLE OF A PIMP

CHAPTER 8
WHAT PIMPS AND PROSTITUTES THINK OF SOCIETY

Society flatly refuses to probe beneath the surface to try to understand the plight of the pimps and prostitutes. Society is ignorant of the facts concerning this lifestyle. Society has become the judge, jury, and the executioner and if every American citizen felt that way, then no one is really safe.

Usually, the pimps and prostitutes are the scapegoats and considered the scum of the earth. But will the real scum of the earth please stand? Is it the child molesters, rapists, hired killers, children murderers, mother killers, drug peddlers, pimps, prostitutes or is it society?

The male who scorns the pimp is himself the hypocrite pimp.

The female who looks down on the girls that take "pay for play" is worse off because if she had sexually dated another man while still married, she's considered a *"daughter of the night"* which labels her a *"hypocrite harlot"* according to the biblical scriptures.

So what are the real ingredients of our society? If there was any way possible to take a nationwide survey of all penal and correctional facilities to determine how many pimps or prostitutes are incarcerated for rape, murder, child molestation or selling drugs, the score would be 98 to 2 in favor of the pimps and prostitutes. Pimps don't do things like that. It is the so-called good guys who commit those type of heinous crimes.

In the future, say in the year 2001, laymen will understand that the woman only belongs to him for a short while, not forever or until death do they part.

When this is understood then, there will be less wife murders.

There will be the understanding that there will be three marriages for both parties. The first one is for love and romance, the second one will represent sexual companionship and the third will represent all combined.

Pimps have known about the future all the while. That is how far ahead of society they are. The *layman* is under the impression that when he and his mate, wife or girlfriend, are in bed in the nude and pull the sheet tent-fashion over their heads and she tells him that everything he sees under there is his forever, he thinks it is his for real. He believes her and goes as far as to kill her if she tells someone else the same thing. But pimps know better.

Pimps and prostitutes are just two loving people trying desperately to make each other happy in this confused world of selfishness. They are also trying to be companions to each other. To succeed in what is considered a legal marriage, the participants have to be compatible. That is why pimps mostly marry in the heart. Four years is a term and after four years, each can go their separate ways or re-elect their same mate for another term.

The prostitute doesn't want to be bothered with a layman unless there is money involved. She has the insight to know that the trick unfortunately could have been her man and he's out buying sex when he could take that money and buy the baby some shoes.

A pimp doesn't want to be bothered with the ordinary working woman. First, he has to beg a square for a date, take her to dinner, wine and dine her, bring her candy, flowers and other gifts, make her appear as a queen in public by opening car doors, pulling out her chair, and resting her coat. The bill is all on him and he probably gets turned down when it comes to the sex department; the old familiar adage *I don't go to bed on the first date.*

The prostitute is just the opposite. The prostitute serves two purposes simultaneously. She makes the married man or a man without a sex mate very happy. No doubt he gets sexual pleasure that he probably doesn't get at home, if nothing more than variety. At the same time, she makes her pimp happy in various ways -companionship, love, sex and finance.

Twenty five percent of marriages are based strictly on sex and after a four-year term, if the marriage lasts that long, at least one of the participants becomes bored with the same old sex routine. Then comes the divorce, separation or split.

If only the participants could sometimes change sex partners, there is no doubt that their marriage could last longer. Society has setup guidelines that make human beings very uncomfortable. The ones who setup the guidelines can't live faithfully by them either. Because the flesh is too weak and the temptation is too great.

What makes the upper-class pimp tick? The same thing that makes other kings tick in various fields - GOD. There are but a chosen few. Pimping is something that more men, believe it or not, women too, than one could imagine have tried at least one time or another. It's amazing how much pimps are envied and looked upon with scorn -if society only knew how pimps think of laymen and how he pities them for not having the strength and courage to live the way they truly feel as long as it doesn't interfere with someone else's life.

The king pimp cares less about guidelines leading him; even those who made the laws do not abide by them. Because being a king pimp, there is never strain or stress on him. The glory of having a group of young, lovely dolls surrounding him at all times, showering him with expensive gifts, love, travel, etc., is beyond reproach. A king pimp is the manager, producer and the director and the prostitute is the STAR. The tricks are her fans and they must pay admission fees before she performs.

Society teaches that if you accept money for sex, you are labeled a *prostitute* (that's to the layman's advantage-free sex). But turn the record over and when you have sex for pleasure (free) you are labeled a *human bitch*.

The female realizes at a very young age that she is something special and that she was born with a meal and transportation ticket -some take advantage of it and some have the *advantage* taken of them - that is where the pimp comes in.

CHAPTER 9
PIMPS AND MADAMS VENDETTA

God created all men and women equal with a gift or talent and an open mind. Often the unfortunate mind is like beautiful flowers that grow wild; deprived of rain, sunshine, care and cultivation. The uncultivated mind is like a wild flower; it usually gets trampled and just dies away. Some of the stronger flowers survive the trampling and are plucked and vased to live the same as some strong minds.

The whorehouse madams are the strong minds behind the trampled and uncultivated minds. As a rule, a whorehouse madam has paid her dues in the world of prostitution and her sex service is no longer marketable; it is now her time to benefit from her past experiences and reap the fruits of her labor.

Everyone has experienced hunger. But there are some that have experienced hunger and didn't know how they were going to eat. It should be known by all what it is like to be reared in a ghetto -whether it be white, black or any other race. In that way, society would have a better understanding about the life of a prostitute or pimp.

Being born poor is a living hell. To have to wait until you die and go to heaven before you can have some milk and honey while society is having theirs now, makes one wonder. Some people have to scratch and claw trying to get their milk and honey here on earth.

It has been said that all women are potential prostitutes, if the occasion presents itself. If there is no food, milk, shoes or clothing for the babies and someone offers a supplement, it's a wonder what one will do.

Prostitution is the oldest profession in the world

and is not considered a crime in most areas of the world. In the USA, these activities used to be a disgrace to the relatives of the participants, but even that has changed as the older generations die and the influence of the church begins to wane. Today, the art of flesh for sale is simply looked upon as *just a way of life,* and not only in the ghettos. Prostitution is a million dollar a year production. That is not a lot of money only to the prostitute, but to almost everybody. As stated earlier, there are various types of prostitutes. They have a thousand faces; from housewives to the street walkers.

It's sometimes revolting to hear society discuss a field that they have only read about. The *do-gooders* will never really know the truth concerning prostitution until they come down from their pedestals and take a glance.

The poor, ugly, uncultivated, uneducated, white and black women have to take the streets for it - whether it's raining, sleeting, storming or snowing. That's hard work and extremely dangerous. While the pretty black and white women are safely protected from harm and the law, in a sauna, house of pleasure, brothel, exclusive hotel or whorehouse, etc.

Very seldom does society ever hear or read about one of these places being interfered with, raided or busted. Everybody gets a piece of the pie. To really pacify the public, the police target the daughters of the nights.

The truth is, society has a neat way of covering up distasteful situations such as high class drugs and prostitution with its headquarters in the suburbs. The only ones who get crucified are the ghetto people. It is conceivable that the ghettos are the jungles but it is home to one that was reared there. There is a jungle code *"survive"*, which well-off Americans would hardly understand. Drugs, prostitution, burglary, robbery, rape, murder, cut throats and bandits will exist as long as there is a ghetto. It grows in the suburbs. Residents of the ghetto don't have the financial resources to purchase wholesale guns or other firearms and drugs. They are not in a financial position to promote prostitution from coast to coast like mackmen can afford to do.

There are many whorehouses all over the world and the only type that the naive, uneducated can learn a little about are the low level ones.

When a wild flower makes her debut in the world of prostitution, the war between the whorehouse madam and the pimp commences. Vendettas swell, in the same manner a prosecuting attorney has for the defense attorney; they both are trying to win. Rather than have one of the five worse pimps, the wild flower is better off with the madam. It's far safer for her. Otherwise, she should have a pimp if he treats her good and fair. Another woman cannot explain to her what a pimp can do, because they have different feelings toward her. There is a thin line between love and infatuation, hot and cold, sane and insane, love and hate, glad and sad and whorehouse madams and pimps.

Regardless of what your talents are, even in prostitution, if an individual does not have an agent, manager, or pimp, she'll only get half of the dollar when the whole dollar could be hers. The house madam serves the prostitute almost in the same respect. She takes forty percent of the prostitutes earnings, some places take as much as fifty percent. The madam is getting her cut for *protection and connection*. It appears to the not knowing public that the pimp gets paid for nothing. But there is no institution that one can attend without paying fees or dues. The pimp teaches her what the schools, colleges, universities and churches forgot to teach, - how to fight in the trenches. When the curtains are pulled, the lights dimmed, the storm has blown over - she will have his comforting arms to protect her.

There are some decent whorehouse madams

that will play fair with a novice. Then there is the witch and she's a real bitch! She does to a new girl what some house madams had done to her in the beginning stages of her career. That is where the pimp would come in.

Whorehouse madams have their schemes and methods just as in any other profession. Most whorehouse madams take advantage of new, fresh, young girls in an effort to try to keep all the money in her house.

"Baby, you can make a lot of money if you stay here with me and do like you are told. You don't have to give your money to a man. You can spend it on yourself. You can buy your own clothes, jewelry, etc.," the madam will advocate. All these things are taught to a young prostitute when she first enters a house with a *witch* for a madam.

As soon as the madam finds out what she needs, wants, or what her weaknesses are, whether it's clothes, jewelry, booze or drugs, the madam will have her mackman to provide it at a large profit.

"You really don't have to pay a pimp for sex when men are constantly walking in here with $50 or $100 wrapped around their penises," the girl is taught.

A pimp and his whore will really have to be together to overcome all that she is going to endure in a house like this and still want to be with her man. If the wild flower still sticks to her pimp, then he gets in the way of the house madam's plans. This is one of the reasons why a whorehouse madam and a pimp have such a vendetta toward each other.

Some madams charge for towels, soap, rent, cooking privileges and sometimes ask them to sexually entertain their special friends and law enforcement officers for free. But pimps will not permit such activities and will quickly find another house.

Some whorehouse madams are on the same level with the houseman of a gambling establishment, trying to round up all the money. The whorehouse madam is just a female pimp. There is usually a mackman behind all whorehouse madams. She's usually old and afraid to be out in the world alone. She can't whore anymore and she gets pressed for money by her mackman.

She will tell the girls that work from her brothel that the mackman is not a pimp, he's a businessman and that he doesn't accept her money (a myth). He does accept her money and she is glad to have someone to accept it. Real macho-men, he-men, do not accept money from a woman. He usually has a good job, supports his family and spends some time with the whores for a variety of purposes and reasons.

There are different types of madams. There are some who are strictly business. They seem to do a lot better than the witch types because they realize that the pimp is the one sending the whores to their houses and the wild flowers must have liked him or loved him to be there in the first place. When the whore gets back to him, she's going to explain what type of person the madam is. If she (the madam) is foul, they find her another house to work out of.

So the trampled wild flower lives on. As long as time exists, there will be beautiful wild flowers. For any girl that has been converted into a prostitute and worked in a brothel, the height of her ambitions is to become a madam. So she goes through life waiting and wishing for the day when they can call her **MADAM**.

There have been saloon girls as long as there have been saloons. While it wasn't becoming for a man to be the head of a brothel, the idea was born to put another more experienced woman in charge. So the mackmen would stay in the background and handle the gambling and drinking end of it, he'd put his oldest woman to watch the pretty, young wild flower entertain the customers. Thus, the madam was born.

In the early stages of prostitution, things went along smoothly in saloons, brothels, and houses of pleasure. This was before pimps and gigolos were discovered. Since the discovery of pimps, madams have been confronted with various types of difficulties and pimps became their competition. Today pimps and whorehouse madams have a potent vendetta toward each other. They are in the same business - peddling flesh - and none is in love with their competition. In certain cases, a house of prostitution works in the very best interest of young, wild flowers and all others that are involved. It has its advantages and disadvantages. It all depends on the madam of the house.

CHAPTER 10
FIFTY-TWO VERSIONS OF PIMPS

There are fifty-two distinct versions of the pimps. Of the entire fifty-two (52) versions, there are five lowest forms and the worse type for any female to come in contact with. The ones that are responsible for society's negative outlook on all pimps. These are the ones that the other 47 versions wish they could tar and feather and hang by the neck until death. They are not fit to live among civilized people.

It takes many different ingredients to bake a cake ... many patches of cloth to complete a quilt ... many different types of people to complete the world. I sincerely believe that normal minded people should be intelligent enough to know that there are some bad individuals in all walks of life.

The pimp game was created with good intentions to serve as a mating game. I blame society for certain things that happen, especially to young, naive girls. They teach sex education, conception of a child, child-birth but refuse to teach a student how **NOT** to come in contact with a person that may possibly ruin her life forever.

Psychologists, sociologists or psychiatrists may research as long as they desire but my belief is that you first must experience a field before becoming an expert in that field.

Any subject not discussed in classrooms or group sessions by someone who has experienced the subject matter will forever remain a mystery. How would a young, naive, uneducated girl know what to do or expect when she is confronted by a villain unless someone teaches her about the subject?

For the first time in history, it's being revealed. You will find the listing of fifty-two (52) versions and definitions of pimps on the following pages.

1. THE KING PIMP

The king pimp is the boss of them all. With seven or eight women, it is just one big happy family. They are all "wives-in-law" and this they must understand. *The bigger the band, the sweeter the music.* When the question arises as to who is number one with him, the line begins to form with the one with the biggest bankroll. They must get along as though they are sisters. When their tempers start to fly and become uncontrollable, he must be able to handle the problem with *the greatest ease and finesse;* not with an iron fist but with diplomacy. It's usually something minute or mundane such as who's supposed to wash his back or who is next to buy him the new automobile. The king pimp rests, dresses, reads the funnies, counts the money and when he so desires, gets the honey. His hobbies are usually golfing, sporting events and, of course, shopping.

With seven or eight women under one roof, he must have the unique ability to handle their delicate minds gently, like long-stemmed roses, candy, with tender love and care. Instead, a layman or society makes an attempt to criticize a king pimp who can control seven or eight female minds at one time, when the average man can't control one,- they should be putting him in the hall of fame. I'm here to tell you, I'm a living witness.

2. THE NATURAL PIMP

He is uninspired, unmotivated. He is a natural - but that is not his desire. He was probably raised by a religious family. Listening to his family, especially his mother, who wants him to be like his father say to him, *"Boy if you think enough to sleep with a woman, then you should think enough of her to marry her and get a job to support her."* Some whores would give their right arm to just play in his lovely head of hair, but the pimp God is beckoning one way and the whores and prostitutes are pulling another. He is a very complexed man. He is dealing with an inner-self and he is not strong enough to break the bond of his family. He has no strain or stress of women wanting to make a pimp out of him, but you must realize it took a male and female to create a human being and he is half of each, which makes him an individual. All he would need is a motivator or an encourager. That is your Natural Pimp.

3. THE GENTLEMAN PIMP

The gentleman pimp must stay poised, calm, and in complete control at all times. His mannerisms and behavior are above reproach. He handles a lady in almost the same fashion as a gigolo. He renders escort services. His word is his bond. He greets ladies with flowers and candies. He is the reason why some blacks think there are black gigolos. But, if that's true, they sure are playing on a low scale because the black boy just does not have a large enough arena in which to mack and gigolo, that is strictly a white boy's turf. Don't get me wrong; blacks can pimp harder than lightning can bump a stump (Pimping is something that is considered small change). Long ago this was all that was left for a black to do. Blacks didn't get started in prostitution and pimping until after the freeing of the slaves.

The slave masters always exploited the slave woman but once she was free, she started getting paid for what she used to give away or that which was taken from her.

There are no Black gigolos and mack-men. But the gentleman pimp comes pretty close.

4. HIGH-CLASS PIMP

The high-class pimp is always the trend-setter. When a mack-man needs a front-man in a black neighborhood, the high-class pimp is usually the one that he will choose. They say he is more intelligent than the others -whoever they call the others. He usually opens a classy or fancy night spot which brings him great respect among his peers. Sometimes he makes another move and become his own boss through the help of some of the fast women he has met while running the show for the mackman. He is usually the first to break the ice in neighborhoods that say "no Blacks allowed or wanted". After he opens the doors, then comes the Black doctors and lawyers who try to run him out. But the upper-class or high-class pimp is in a class by himself.

5. PROCURER

The procurer is harmless. He is either a bellboy, cab driver, doorman, bartender, waiter or shoe shine boy. The procurer is anyone who will find a trick or a john for a whore or prostitute. He usually plants two or three whores or prostitutes at his apartment, then he hits the streets, whether it is raining, sleeting or snowing. Weather does not stop the procurer; he realizes the he has something at home that will sell when cotton and corn would not, - it is no seasonal product.

All he wants is his cut. He gets forty percent of what he sends or brings in. You can always find the procurer wherever a major event is or any place where there's a gathering of men. None of the women are his; although, he sometimes receives sexual favors from them. He will pay forty percent of her bond if the law ever gets in the picture; he is a real hustler and is as important to a pimp, trick, john, whore or prostitute as a paddle is to a canoe.

6. THE SIX-GIRL PIMP

The Six Girl Pimp is so close to the high-class and king pimp that he has to be reckoned with. He is the leading contender for the King Pimp's title. When a pimp can have seven whores, one to represent each day of the week, he is rated in the King Pimps's category. If he can handle them properly, his merits are weighed against the one that is incumbent. The news will spread and other pimps and whores do the deciding as to who is the real king pimp. It is amazing how society and the laymen look at the pimp situation. But it is big business and one cannot make a joke of a million dollar a year production. This money buys property, homes, cars, jewelry, vacations, leisure, sex, companionship or whatever, it is you desire.

There was an ex-first lady who asked her future husband for $30,000,000 before marriage and $20,000 to $30,000 a month for pocket money. Now if that's not sugar-coated prostitution, I'd love to know what is!

7. THE MOTHER PIMP

As far as female pimps are concerned, the Mother Pimp is the boss. She has been there and back; she has all the answers because she has been asked all the questions. She spreads her wild oats in the shuffle, got stuck with one or more beautiful daughters and had to raise them all alone. When she was young, she had some form of a pimp and he stepped away and left her to carry the load. But the vow that she made, made her a Mother Pimp - what happened to her will never happen to her daughter or daughters. I always say, "a house is no stronger than the foundation that it is built on." The daughters become well-trained and well-informed. They learn that you don't give away what is good enough to sell; neither marriage nor money, and also don't marry the poor. They are taught to get yours first; *because after the thrill comes the chill.* The daughter or daughters know how to deal with men. She is taught to get all you can from the dirty bastards and don't ever give them a dime. Get all you can and take it home to mummy.

8. THE WHOREHOUSE PIMP

At the beginning, it was the mack-men overseeing the whorehouses but that became obsolete. Since then, it has become very popular to have the madam over the girls which transforms her into a whorehouse pimp. They vary in the percentage of a whore's earnings, some take forty percent, some sixty percent and some half. They charge for the rooms, towels, soap, and food. The house has standard tricks that are regulars and the house charges for the *protection and con-*

nections.

In certain brothels, there are a few male whore-house pimps who have the same type of protection and connection that the madam has plus also plenty of sexual favors. Some of the girls may belong to him and that's so much the better as he is constantly trying to improve his stable and tries to steal every other pimp's woman that is sent there. So a pimp must have his girls properly trained before sending her to a house where there is only one stud.

9. DOPE FIEND PIMP

This is the kind of pimp that "Iceberg Slim" said he was. A pimp with a drug habit is a hopeless cause. Any pimp of consequence may take a blow of cocaine but never hypodermic needles; that is strictly a *"No No"*. This type of pimp seldom sees the inside of a jail cell. One thing that you don't have to worry about where a dope fiend is concerned is he is not going to rape any-one too fast. He may rip his mother off but sex is the furthest thing from his mind. Having sex when he is high is like crying and laughing at the same time. When he and his woman have sex, it is just something to do. Those little white grains are their sex, food, and the utmost goal in their pathetic life. They may be a bee in the policeman's bonnet because what they want is their fix and each other's company.

10. THE POLICE PIMP

Officer Friendly gets a lot of good shots and some top action. He meets all the good whores and prosti-tutes first and because of his position, he is in demand for protection reasons. Which street whore would not want that type of protection? When a slick whore gets a bully or a gorilla pimp and gets tired of him, she chooses *Officer Friendly* and when Officer Splivengate (a name commonly given to police by pimps), gets her, he cops lock, stock and barrel and blocks anyone else from tampering with his property. He has it all to himself until she leaves the town or another Officer Splinvengate plucks him off. But the officers better take a warning from one who knows a whore. If she decides to have a change of heart, she will have him walking a beat or fired.

11. THE BLACKMAILING PIMP

The Blackmailing Pimp is a Bastard with a capital B. He'll discover something on a woman that he knows she cannot afford to have exposed and threatens her with it unless she does whatever he demands. For instance, he may get her drunk or give her a mickey and then he calls a bunch of sex starved bums and let them have sex with her while he snaps pictures of her in different engaging sex positions. When she returns to sobriety, he shows her the photos and tells her that she asked for it. He then threatens to expose her to her husband, boyfriend, family or who ever, unless she does what he wants her to do. He wants her to become a prostitute and there is no telling how long she will have to submit to his demands as long as he has the photos; which he will never release. That is the only hold he has on her. Sometimes women never want to go home again and stay with the blackmailing pimp as his whore.

12. THE FLAT-BACK PIMP

The Flat-Back Pimp is the one that really doesn't have anything to tell a whore. He is like the *chili pimp* who was just trying to survive his hotel fare and his meal ticket, when he made his street debut and got a whiff of the pimp game. He makes a fast track back to the little girl that he had left behind; because two to one, he got her pregnant. She thinks she is in love with him and is willing to do whatever he asks. He tells her what he heard in the streets but it is all new to her. "Baby, if you really love me then what you have been giving away, we are going to start selling." That is about as far as he can go in the pimp game. She no doubt will be flat-backing it the rest of her life unless God intervenes. This is one of the lowest forms of prostitution.

13. THE PREACHER PIMP

The Preacher Pimp should not surprise anyone. He has been doing it from the beginning of time and the law cannot touch him. He pimps on women, men and children. He rates with the best. Most of the time their opening sermon is I want twenty good men to come to the front and put $20 in the basket. It is unbelievable how many men race to be a "good man." One preacher pimp got rich just by saying **"Black is Beautiful."** He moved to Pill Hill the following week.

14. THE WHORE'S PIMP

The Whore's Pimp is too foxy to deal with anything but a whore. He doesn't care to be bothered with the high-class prostitutes, etc. When it comes to acquiring illicit money, a whore (mud kicker) is hard to beat. The prostitute usually works on the inside where there are mostly half standard policies. The whore can work any place at anytime and practices a bit of the con game. The whore doesn't have a set price.

"What do you want for your money and how much are you going to spend?" These are the type of questions the whore will ask first.

What the trick wants is just what he gets. She knows that as soon as he gets her in a bedroom he is going to ask for more and she is smart enough to charge him for all the extras. Kissing, breast fondling, real-like loving, raising her legs over her head, etc.. In most cases, a prostitute will take one price and give up all the rest. This is one of the reasons why a whore's pimp is not going to deal with a prostitute. Different strokes for different folks.

15. THE GYPSY PIMP

The Gypsy Pimp is one of a kind. He is in the category of a king pimp. He is king in the *world of the gypsies*. He never has any trouble with any of his females because the gypsies have only their men. Men talk of the different type races of women, that they have known sexually but you never hear them mention having experienced the love of the gypsy girl and rarely does anyone lie about it. If a gypsy woman or girl should disappear overnight, gypsies come from far and near to help capture her. Her punishment is not confirmed, but that is a black day in the world of gypsies.

16. THE WHITE GIRL PIMP

The White Girl Pimp seeks out only white girls for a variety reasons. First, she's considered an easy prey. Second she has a wider area in which to play. She definitely serves as a window dressing when dealing with a black. If she decides, she can reach in her treasure chest and women have mighty precious stones in these chests, but white girls gems seem to be more valuable. The black man has no strain or stress in getting money. All he has to do for money is to look on his dresser. Financially, having a white girl compared to a black is like leaving hell and entering heaven. No more fussing, arguing, and wanting for the essentials of life.

In the back of a white girl's mind is sympathy for the black man because of the way her people have oppressed him. On the other hand, a white girl's pimp refuses to deal with a black girl, saying, "I'd rather see a black bitch go to the electric chair than see a white lady cry." He says that for the white girl's benefit; he knows that "Sapphire" can see through that thin shit he's pulling and is not about to give up her ADC check. The uglier the black girl is, the prettier the white girl usually is. Does the contrast make a difference? A white girl pimp's pimping ability is questionable.

17. THE BLACK GIRL PIMP

The Black Girl Pimp is shrewd enough not to look for the woman he wants but for the ones that want him. He believes that all cunts will sell and he is willing to take all that the others don't want. He can stand next to any pimp and get top recognition because they know he only wants what they don't want. He is no major threat. He stays clean and keeps a pocket full of money and does not go out of his way to look for a whore. He knows that his kind will come to him. They will have to approach him. "If she is a she, give her to me."

18. THE PROPERTY-OWNING PIMP

The Property Owning Pimp can provide shelter for a poor out-of-doors whore who has no place to live. That is the main stick he fights with. She is glad to move in with him under the impression that someday she may end up as part owner of the property. However, it is a two to one bet that his property is incorporated and she could not touch it. What she doesn't realize is that he had it when she came and he will have it when she leaves. While she is with him, she must produce on the promise that he is going to make her a shareholder. She must walk the chalk line. If she does not, she will quickly find herself without a home, back on the streets in worse circumstances than she was before she came with him. How can some women be so stupid?

19. THE GORILLA PIMP

The Gorilla Pimp is usually a big guy with a sinister look on his face. In size, he is large but very small in the brain and heart department. He gets by on his physical attributes, but if you dig below the surface, you will find that his heart is not as big as a mustard seed. He is a tester. He will test you to find out if you are afraid of his size and when he finds out you'll get in his ass, he becomes your supposed friend. Feed him but feed him with a long handle spoon. That bastard will ask for your car first, your money, and then your woman. He will reach at your prestige if your guard is down and will get it if he is allowed half a chance.

They make pretty good bouncers and that is about all. He is another one of the worse kind of pimps. He whips, kicks and is death on a whore but thinks twice before tackling another man. He thinks his size will get him over but he forgets that there is an equalizer for size.

20. BUSINESSMAN PIMP

The Businessman Pimp is a rarity. He learns from his experience in life, the true value of a dollar and how to multiply it. The business man pimp, pimps as hard and fast as he can, in order to use the pimp money as a stepping stone to set up legal business ventures. He saves as much as he can, trying to get in a position so he won't have to pimp anymore. He strives hard to get into some other form of business. As soon as he gets the amount of money he wants, he is through with pimping, (at least on the low-level).

21. THE WORKING PIMP

It is a customary thing to see a woman put on her mask (makeup) but one should see the working pimp put his on. The ugliest man in the world thinks he is handsome when he puts on a new suit. The working pimp puts on his best and comes out in the daytime, providing he works at night and vice versa. To the average woman, it is hard to tell the difference between the working pimp and the real pimp. A real whore does not want her man to work and would die if she thought that she was paying a layman. A working pimp does not have enough time to put into a whore to be a successful pimp in the game of lost love. He takes the money the whore gives him, pockets it, spends a night with her, gets up and leaves while the whore is still sleeping and gets home in time to be back on that job on time-he is just meddling.

22. THE HUSBAND PIMP

There is an old saying that it would be easier to make a race horse out of a donkey than it would be to make a whore out of a housewife. When a man marries a whore he is blessed. They are supposed to make the best wives. Sex does not excite them anymore unless it is with her man. It is strictly about the green stuff with her. No yokel can bring her a game that she has not heard of or played before. She keeps her body excessively clean and free of disease. She specializes in hygiene, body, dental, perfumes, etc. There are only two kinds of whores a clean whore and an unclean whore. But if she is first class, no one and I mean no one, has to tell her to visit her doctor. She will do this automatically, at least once a month, to make sure that she is in top shape. That is why at a massage parlor, whorehouse or any other place of illicit sex pleasures where there are standard prices, you won't have to concern yourself with contracting a disease.

Street walkers, flat backs, dope addicts, and car hoppers are usually the ones that carry the sexually transmitted diseases and at this point in time, the deadly AIDS. Most of them are filthy. But the husband pimp is safe and at home safely tucked away and all he has to do is keep looking on the dresser.

23. THE SISSY PIMP

The Sissy Pimp is a young, handsome, fresh guy who is supported only by wolves (homosexuals). He knows where to get some money at any time. He is very seldom seen in the company of females because if you keep dealing, you might start shuffling one day. The homosexuals have a lot of tricks for the naive young man. Sometimes the strong outwit the weak. He is ashamed of his counterparts in public and they usually have an understanding. But there are some that will get so carried away over the affair that they can't stand to see the youngster talk to a woman and better not see him talk to another homo.

24. THE HENPECKED PIMP

The Henpecked Pimp woman loves him very much and realizes that she can handle him. She tried the same techniques on other men and it did not work so she tries to hold on to what she's got. A henpecked pimp is very difficult to find. Wherever he goes she wants to go. She doesn't want him to associate with too many men. He is the mild-mannered type that won't talk too much but thinks deeply. He is in love with his woman but wishes she would give him breathing room. She is more experienced than he is and she is not taking any chances. But she is not going to let him starve.

25. THE RENEGADE PIMP

There is not much difference between him and the transporting pimp. He will do his kidnaping and still hang around the city where he lives. He is one of the worst types and somewhat the blame for the way

in which society looks at all other pimps. He snatches
girls off the streets and threatens them with violent acts.
He keeps them for a certain length of time and releases
them, soon to get another one. He makes them whore
for him while he trails behind them and after she has
made a certain amount of money, she is free to go. He
never has one whore too long because he is not in demand.

26. THE SATURDAY NIGHT PIMP

The Saturday Night Pimp comes out once a
week. Dressed sharp enough to shave with. You only
have one night to be bothered with him and that's Saturday. He will have his pimp uniform on and his hat
cocked ace-duce and it's hard to tell him from the real
McCoy. He is just out to fool some old crazy lonely whore
for whatever he can get from her, including sex. He may
even spend the night with her but Sunday, he is back
home getting ready to go to work the next day. He tells
his wife he had been playing poker with the boys all
night and when she sees the little money that the whore
gave him, she is cool.

27. THE WEAK PIMP

The Weak Pimp is the real pretty boy. In fact, he
is so pretty he should have been a girl. He out-shines
all of his girls and instead of being their protector, *they
protect him*. He is scared to death and his women are
his strength. If he is an octoroon with colored eyes and
curly hair, he is probably surrounded by those big dark-
skinned, husky women. He reminds them of the dolls
that they never had as children and they would kill a

brick for him. If a gangster, bully, or gorilla pimp comes
on the scene and says anything, the weak pimp grins,
whether it's funny or not and if it wasn't for the strength
of his women, the other pimps would eat him alive.

28. THE GANGSTER PIMP

The Gangster Pimp is Humphrey Bogart, James
Cagney and Al Capone all wrapped up in one --in his
mind. He wears his hat to one side and hardly ever
smiles. He tells his woman all type of lies, such as, he is
working for the Mafia or some syndicate of white hoods.
They believe him. They'll go and get him as much
money as they can with their sex services. He tells them
he's going to a gangster meeting with the mob. When
they leave to go back to work, he heads to a crap game
or after-hours joint and tries gambling. If he wins, he
acts big when he sees his woman again; if he loses, he
is vile and tough. They are under the impression that if
they don't do what he tells them, they might end up in
the trunk of a car. That is his lifestyle of pimping, but
the only gangsters he knows are the ones he sees on
the television or at the movies.

29. THE MINOR PIMP

The Minor Pimp is also one of the worst types
of the 52 versions of pimps. He chooses under-age girls.
Sixty-five percent of the minor pimps are usually short
and thin, looks good, and dresses young. He is a teen-
age girl's worse nightmare. He is 26 to 30 years old but
appears to be much younger. I've known some pimps
to turn girls out at the tender age of 9 years old. It's sad
to say, but it's true. Beware of old men with gym shoes,
jump-suits and their caps turned backwards.

30. THE OCCASIONAL PIMP

The Occasional Pimp is the independent type. He already has a good income from some source and could care less whether he ever got a dime from a whore. But the glory of knowing he can beg her, if that would be his desire, feeds his petty ego. He is only seen on certain occasions -he is really just another meddler.

31. THE LOVING PIMP

The Loving Pimp and his woman are desperately in love with each other in the same respect that a high school boy and girl are in love. They see no one else but each other. They are just two loving people trying to make each other happy and as comfortable as possible. The money she gets is strictly for their survival. She is so indoctrinated in her man that nothing a John or a trick could say or do would change her mind. She is in love with him and he is in love with her.

32. THE ENTERTAINING PIMP

The Entertaining Pimp, he has many forms or talent, i.e., singing, dancing or playing a musical instrument. If he is struggling in the chit'lin circuit and meets a daughter of the night with stars in her eyes, he can lead her to the end of the earth; just by telling her they are headed for Hollywood and that one day they are going to walk on Broadway. She will work her hands to the bone, lying, whoring, stealing and what-ever else it takes to make him happy and to keep him living in the style that an artist is supposed to live. She provides him with luxury automobiles, jewelry, expensive clothes and a big bankroll. As the years pass, she slowly begins to see that she is not going to Hollywood and neither is he.

33. STUDENT PIMP

The Student Pimp is the academic-minded young man. He has decided to become a medical doctor, but due to financial reasons, he is in doubt. If he is lucky enough to meet a lady of the evening, and can lie fairly well, that is, good enough to make her believe that if she should support him until he completes medical school, that his future lies with her as far as his becoming a physician. It is a good bet that finances won't be too big a problem. But what does a doctor want with a whore?

34. THE ATHLETE PIMP

The Athlete Pimp is usually liked by women because of their muscles. Generally, they are supposed to be in excellent condition and can give out sex abundantly. Whether he is a promising football player, basketball player, boxer, or baseball player, he knows how to lie about his career and all of the good things that will follow. Her reward will come if she can hold him up until his ship comes in. The poor whore would work in the rain, sleet or snow to see that he maintains his status and gets the proper training, waiting for the day to show. And if it shows, he would outgrow her and become too big for her. It is like a young girl who lives with a man until she gets too old and then ask him to marry her - for what?

35. THE TRANSPORTING PIMP

The Transporting Pimp is crazy to anybody with any sense! He goes from state to state, picking up girls, kidnaping and gangstering them. He takes them across state lines even after realizing that this brings in the FBI. **He goes to the penitentiary more than any other of the 52 pimps.** But that's his style of pimping and you can't pan success. It pays off for him because he knows if he can get her away from home and family, she'll have to depend solely on him. He is either dumb, stupid, or has a lot of just plain raw nerve.

36. THE DUMB PIMP

The Dumb Pimp is easily led. Usually the other pimps know he's dumb. If he has a nice little dish and the rest of the pimps are trying to knock him (steal his woman), they just tell him that she is not bringing home enough money for the way she looks and that if he had her, he'd break that bitch's arms. And besides, they wouldn't let a woman talk to them like the dumb pimp's woman talks to him. The dumb pimp will go for real and break her arm. Then the slick pimp gets her, nurses her back to health and keeps her.

37. THE COMMON SNAKE PIMP

The Common Snake Pimp is almost as bad as the gorilla pimp, he stinks. He tries to play the game and escape the name that he's trying to snake something. If he catches a whore in between whoring, he keeps trying to reform her. He pretends that he's not a pimp and how much he dislikes any man that would take money from a female. Then he reaches at her from the borrowing tip. That's his style of pimping. He is the kind that will call a working man's wife and tell on him. He'll sneak around and tell a pimp where there's something on him. He's just what they named him, a SNAKE PIMP. He is the kind of snake that the King snakes like to destroy.

38. THE SIDEWALK PIMP

The Sidewalk Pimp is to be reckoned with; his quality, prestige, and pride is evident. He was not born with a silver spoon in his mouth. He has no visible means of income, he doesn't sell drugs or do anything that might get him in trouble with the law. His motto is *"ABC, ALWAYS BE CLEAN."* If a broad chooses him it's for him only, not for what's he's got, and he captures as many women as the man with the dope bag. He believes that if a woman doesn't dig you in overalls she won't dig you in a tuxedo. Just keep your body clean and she'll buy you a suit, if she likes you.

39. THE GIGOLO PIMP

The Gigolo Pimp is a white boy. When you hear a white refer to himself, as a pimp, which is seldom heard, he is cheapening himself. Why should he want to be a pimp when the pimp only has a backyard to play and the gigolos and mack-men have the whole world? That's like a white bum asking a black man for a dime to buy a cup of coffee. The gigolo is something special. His mannerism, behavior, dress are all intact. He is usually extremely handsome, immaculate and his time is his own. He serves as a companion, escort -having the techniques to deal with elderly women, elderly wealthy women. Sometimes there is a one night or one week stand with a beautiful young thing. After the affair, they leave it just like they found it. He profits.

40. THE MIXOLOGIST PIMP

The Mixologist Pimp mixes the pimp game with all other games-including drugs. When one looks at the surface, he seems to be straight out pimping. He has plenty field women doing different things. His car is up to par and so are his clothes and jewelry. The grass really looks greener to the naive but when they get over there, it is loaded with dandelions.

41. THE PRODUCER PIMP

The Producer Pimp is either a bellboy, cabdriver, doorman, waiter or anyone who will find a date or trick for a whore or prostitute. He will plant two or three whores in his personal apartment and he hits the streets. If it's raining, sleeting, or snowing, it won't stop the producer. He knows that he has something at home that will sell when cotton won't and he gets forty (40) percent of whatever she brings in. You can always find the producer in public places; he's a real hustler. Some of the women are his, but he can sometimes get as many sexual favors as he likes. He will pay forty (40) percent of her bond if the law ever gets in the picture.

42. THE LESBIAN PIMP

The Lesbian Pimp is like the blind leading the blind. Two females playing the whore and pimp game. In a lot of instances, they do much better than quite a few of the other forms of pimps. At least they are faithful to each other. That's more than can be said about a lot of them. They mind their own business as long as they are not interfered with. They are shooting a double-barrel shotgun in case a John or trick wants to have a party. They are getting paid handsomely for what they do at home for kicks. Usually the dominating woman is a participant.

43. THE IMPERSONATING PIMP

There should be a pimp law forbidding the Impersonating Pimp to exist. He is the kind who hangs around real pimps; hearing, seeing what they say and do and how they react. Then he goes off and practices the ways of the pimp. Iceberg Slim was one of these kind. Although he admitted that he was a dope fiend; he was very successful with the books he wrote, and was instrumental in my writing this book; *"The Sweet Science of Sin."* Some people try to compare Iceberg Slim to me but I'm afraid there would be no contest. I could ask him one question that might damage his brain. But for one to capitalize on what another has lived, is something to think about. King pimps don't shoot drugs. How could a king pimp watch his stable of women when he is sitting somewhere nodding?

44. THE DRUG-PEDDLING PIMP

The Drug-Peddling Pimp is the pimp that the whore and the prostitute can never detect. The whores and prostitutes think that he is a sucker, trick, old fool, when all the time she is the fool. She thinks she is going to get something for nothing, but you get what your hand calls for in the jungle life. The semi-slick whore and prostitute may think that she is reaching for the gold but as soon as she touches it, it turns to SLIME.

The world has become wicked and wiser. The drug peddler is not the fool that the female thinks he is. He is not going to keep throwing rocks at the penitentiary alone. Her assistance is needed. If he goes, she is going too and she just might beat him there.

He is strong, brave and desperate and she's got to be as much woman as he is man. If she wants a share of the profit, she must carry her weight. He would rather not be called a pimp, but a gangster and his woman his moll.

45. THE MACK-MAN PIMP

The Mack-man Pimp is another white boy game, but only because he is in a better financial position, with good prostitution connections from coast to coast. If he should catch a girl of fifteen (15) years of age, when he turns her out, she may be age forty-five (45). When she gets old in one state he exchanges her for one that is new in another state. He floats her from state to state until her service is no longer in demand. The mack-man put no claim on any woman as far as his personal life is concerned. It is strictly business with him, as I said before it cheapens a white boy's status to be called a pimp. A pimp is a derivative of a pimple, thus something small. Why should they reach for something small when they can reach for big things? In other words why take half the dollar when the whole dollar can be yours?

The following are four pimps that are not in the prostitution category. When a person is referred to as a pimp, the layman is under the false impression that their women are either whores or prostitutes. The following group of women don't have to resort to their bodies but their brains.

I'm sorry to say but prostitution is the lowest form of the game but everyone has to start some place. Staying in prostitution forever is like staying in grammar school forever.

46. THE COMMON PIMP

The Common Pimp is the one with the masterpiece lie. He teaches it to his woman, and he is the one that is essential to aiding in derailing society and other laymen in believing that all women who are tutored by pimps are whores and prostitutes. His woman's body is not for sale. It is for him only. Her brain is her weapon, not her body. He would also rather not be called a pimp; to him and his woman, he is not pimping. But any man that accepts money from a woman, pimped that time. No man accepts money from females but pimps. A pure red-blooded man would not dare accept money from a female. That would tear his pride apart. These so-called macho men should get a job and support their females. She is not a whore or a prostitute. Her body belongs to her daddy. He would also rather not be called a pimp fearing what the public might think. He would rather be called *"The Man That Wasn't There."*

47. THE BULLY PIMP

The Bully Pimp comes under the heading of the gorilla pimp. With the exception of size, he's mostly small or short in stature but big as life when it comes to the heart department. His heart makes up for his physical size. He's not afraid of anything especially not big or tall guys. He bullies whores and anybody else that gets in his way. This is his way of proving he is a man and he wants his woman to recognize that. He has a very selected list of tall or big guys that he even likes -so watch out big guys, *Shorty* don't play and he is usually armed.

48. THE WELFARE PIMP

The Welfare Pimp is a big and very popular pimp in the ghetto. His women must have at least four to five children. The women in the ghetto with the most children are the most popular. They are always in demand. If he has at least three women and each one gives him a portion of her welfare check, he can live considerably comfortable according to ghetto living. He is constantly on the prowl, trying to increase his stable. Each woman has her day and gets the chance to spend the day with him on check day.

49. THE PIMP WITH A MISSION

The Pimp With A Mission learns at a very young age, what the odds are. The odds are, that a young man would not earn a large sum of money, and if he does he would not do anything constructive with it. But a pimp with a mission, will pimp with his main focus being to save as much money as possible. He strives to get in a position, whereby he can invest into some form of legal business, so eventually he could get out of the pimp game. He makes a real business out of the game and does what he had in mind in the first place. He'll probably open up a barber shop, bar-b-que joint, a cleaners, etc. If his woman (bottom broad) really goes along with him, he will probably take her along with him. But if she has given him hell in his endeavors, he's subject to drop her and get tight with a complete square. When he gets out of the game, after accomplishing his mission, he gets completely out of the game.

50. THE BLIND PIMP

Although it's hard to believe, the blind pimp may not be able to see, but that has a great bearing on his thinking ability. Whenever you see a blind man sitting on his stool picking his guitar and a pretty girl is sticking out a tin cup to everyone saying *"Help the blind,"* don't be surprised if you see them at the same places you go after the day's pimping is done, at a crap house, shooting dice —it's incredible.

51. THE HYPOCRITE PIMP

The Hypocrite Pimp is almost as bad as the transporting pimp. He stinks. He is another one who tries to play the game and escapes the game at the beginning. He never carries a sign on his back. He is constantly criticizing pimps. He comes like a thief in the night. When a woman realizes that she has been pimped on, it is usually too late. He pretends he is not a pimp and keeps talking about how much he dislikes a pimp or any man that takes money from a woman. All the while, trying to sneak up on something. Then he'll reach at her on a borrowing basis; that is his style of pimping. He'd sneak around and drop drugs in a woman's purse and then tell the police or her boss that she has it. This is to get her fired off her job so she can resort to prostitution with him being her pimp. He is sometimes referred to as a snake pimp and he's the kind that the king snake likes to destroy.

52. THE PREJUDICE PIMP

The Prejudice Pimp is the militant type. He's mad at the white world and he takes it out on the white whore if he's lucky enough to stop one. He will treat the girl of his race fairly decent, but woe and behold the white girl! He keeps his foot in her ass, works her harder, beats the living hell out of her and makes the rest of the white world trained to stay away from niggers!

Chapter 11
THE FIVE WORST TYPES OF WHORES, PROSTITUTES AND PIMPS

The following are brief descriptions of the five worst types of whores and prostitutes.

1. The Outlaw Whore

She has no man. She's the type who is selfish and does not care whether a John or trick gets his money's worth or not. All she wants is to get the money in her hand. She might run away, leaving him hanging. This is one of the reasons many prostitutes are found dead.

2. The Hypocrite

She has no intention of having sex. She wants something for nothing. Her job is to stall the John or trick into a hotel room, bickering over the price while her pimp robs the car. This is because as a rule the trick or John will hide the biggest portion of his money in his car when going to the hotel with a whore. Most of the time he is careless in hiding it and she sees where he puts it. She and her man have certain signals --- beware of her!

3. The Street Walkers

She is contagious. She doesn't usually have adequate cleaning facilities. She usually carries toilet tissues or napkins in her purse for cleaning purposes. She can be hazardous to one's health --- from genital herpes to AIDS.

4. The Drug Addict

The sky is the limit. She is usually sore from abscesses and swollen parts of her body. She is certainly one to beware of, she is dangerous, will do bodily harm. It is sometimes difficult for a layman to tell the difference --- she's very deceptive.

5. Male Prositutes

He will tell the layman that is the wrong time of the month for "her" to have sexual intercourse, but will make oral love to him. If the John or trick reneges, he is subject to a stick-up.

THE FIVE WORST TYPES OF PIMPS

1. FLAT-BACK PIMP

Ronald had courted Shirley since grammer school. She was not an attractive girl but she served Ronald's sexual needs. As an extra boost, Shirley had a 42-inch bosom. Ronald was considered a very good looking dude with his olive complexion and black, curly hair. Shirley was nuts aboout him and Ronald could wrap her around his little finger.

When they started high school, Ronald became very popular with other girls and tried drifting away from Shirley, but she was so infaturated she didn't mind as long as she could see him sometimes. The only time he would give Shirley any attention is when he wanted sex and didn't have any other place to get it.

Once he hit the streets, he started hearing things that he never heard in school, i.e., robbery or stick-up, burglary, pushing dope, pocket picking, fake checks, cutting old ladies' handbags on the subway and pimping.

All the above fascinated Ronald, but he wasn't

good at any of the above games. He tried them all; the only thing he thought he could be successful at was pimping, and he knew the one person he could get to do anything for him ---Shirley.

He took his newly discovered project to Shirley.

"Shirley, you have always told me that you loved me and now is the time to prove it. You know my folks don't give me any money since I left school and everybody has a woman out here but me. I don't want anyone but you and they are getting money for what you are giving away'. Ronald said.

"But only to you." Shirley countered.

"Well baby, let's face it; you know and I know that I can't get all the sex that you have to offer. You just let me get all I can get and we profit from the surplus. That way we can both have some money and some of the nice things in life," Ronald smoothly told Shirley.

"But Ronald, how could you tell me you care about me and want me to let some other men touch me?" Shirley asked.

"Baby, after you take a douche and a good bath, you are all brand new again. If a baby can come out of you, there's not too much harm another man can do by merely having sex with you." Ronald smoothly talked the lines he had heard from other young pimps, with Shirley getting weaker all the time.

"Ronald, I truly love you. You are the only man that I will let make love to me, I just can't do that. Suppose I get pregnant by someone else?" she signed.

Disgusted, Ronald told her, "You could have an abortion, it's free you know."

"Ronald, no I just can't do that, as much as I love you, I just can't, I'm sorry." She said as the tears swelled in her eyes.

"Okay, then I'll tell you what, just forget that you ever knew me."

"He turned and walked away. He didn't call her

for two weeks. Shirley finally called him, but he was
never at home. A month passed and a few nights later
around 10 p.m., while Ronald and some more fellows
were standing on the corner by a neighborhood drug-
store, one of the guys looked down the street and saw
Shirley alone. She was exposing her breast slightly
behind her halter. "Wow! man, look at those tits. That's
enough to run a guy nuts," one of the fellows commented.

Ronald turned around and to his surprise, it was
Shirley. She walked straight up to Ronald and said, "I
changed my mind. If that's what you want me to do, I
guess it's the right thing to do, if you love a person and
I do love you Ronald," she told him.

Ronald put his arms around her and told the
fellows he would see them later, while they stood there
utterly dumbfounded. "Ronald you know I'll have to
leave home and quit school, where are we going to live?
We can't live with your parents," she told him.

"Don't worry about it baby, I'll show you how it
goes," Ronald reassured her.

Once she left, things began to change. Ronald
put her with some real experienced streetwalkers and
flat-backs. They rented a cheap hotel room and
Shirley's big bust sold for her. She brought in about
$200 a week at the beginning and Ronald had become
a flat-back pimp. Later, Ronald raised her quota to $300
a week, then $400, then $500, then $100 a night; telling
her *"If you don't get down, don't come home."*

After associating with the renegade pimps, he
became one. He started beating Shirley with wire hang-
ers, knocking her down in the street, kicking and
bitching if she came home with less than $100 a night.

One night, Shirley came home with $98, two
dollars short of her quota. Ronald was furious and crazy
mad.

"Bitch, you dealing with a pimp. I told you a bill a night and you come stepping your funky ass up here with $98. This ain't no school, school is out bitch. You'd better have my money right or I'm gonna kick your nasty ass."

Much to Shirley's dismay she became pregnant.

"Ronald, I'm pregnant, what must I do? I'm afraid to have an abortion and besides, it's against my religion."

"Bitch, it's not mine and I don't want no trick baby and if you give birth to it, I'll kill it and sell the blood because a pimp's got to live." He said a lot of other slick, pimp talk and walked away.

Shirley had just turned 18 years when she gave birth to the child. Her parents had heard about the pregnancy and went to the hospital to see her and tried to get her to return home. But the devil had a tight grip on her (or maybe it was Ronald). Her parents took the baby.

One day while standing around some older and upper-class pimps, Ronald asked the one that he most admired some questions he wanted answered,

"Well son, I have pimped from coast to coast for forty (40) years on Black, White, Chinese, Mexican, Indian and Puerto Rican women but you youngsters have made a vicious game out of the love game. Pimping is a business, you see son...first you have to learn something constructive yourself and teach it to your women, to keep them in this jungle the rest of your life.

Life itself is about elevation. There are a lot of things a young girl can do because she has a young mind, but you have to learn them first and then teach her and get her out of the streets as quickly as possible. There are more ways to make money other than selling your body." The old pimp told Ronald.

Ronald couldn't understand any of that and waited until Shirley came home at night to eat, pay the hotel bill, and waste the rest unnecessarily. Shirley wished a thousand times that she had not left her comfortable home with her parents and stayed in school, rather than a life in the streets with Ronald. Shirley would go through her pitiful life, selling her body in the streets with no future in sight and unless God intervened, you'll probably find Shirley on Belmont Street on the north-side of Chicago, doing what has become natural to her.

2. TRANSPORTING PIMP

Jennifer was a special child (mentally retarded). Her parents sent her to a special school in Cleveland, Ohio and while she was there she met a group of dropouts. They persuaded her to take a ride with them. She never returned to school and was kidnapped and forced into a life of prostitution.

Jennifer learned well, but by force. The months rolled by with no word of Jennifer and finally the FBI was called in. But still no sign of Jennifer. Her parents would not allow the issue to die. They kept the pressure on the Cleveland authorities and the FBI.

About a year later, Jennifer was arrested in a prostitution ring gathering. When they discovered who she was, the authorities notified her parents. When they came to pick her up, it was too late to deter her feeble mind. Jennifer had become a seasoned prostitute.

Her mother brought her back to Chicago and desperately tried to keep an eye on her and keep her as close to home as possible, but boredom set in and Jennifer began to sneak out and find her way to some kind of male companionship.

She became pregnant and after the baby was born, her mother tried even harder to keep an eye on her, thinking that may be the baby would keep her still. But she told her mother that she wanted to get a job and help take care of her baby. Her mother was in doubt, but Jennifer was of legal age (19 years old), although, she had the mind of a 10 year old. Her mother agreed to her going to the downtown employment office, where she was confronted by one of the worse type of pimp.

He started a conversation with her while she was doing some eye-buying for her baby.

"Hi pretty, how are you doing?" The renegade pimp asked. Jennifer looked up with her Mongoloid features and slightly crossed eyes and said, "Hi, I guess I'm ok, just bored."

"Bored about what?" The pimp asked.

"Life itself," she replied.

"Well, I've got just the thing for a pretty, bored girl like you," the bastard said.

"What?" Jennifer asked.

"Do you smoke reefer? This is dynamite, it's fire, it'll make you forget about your problems," he told her.

"Yeah, I get high." She was being a weak and easy prey. He sweet talked her into following him home to get high."

Once at his house, he talked her into having sex with him and gave her his phone number. She didn't give him hers because she didn't want her mother to find out that she had met what she thought was a nice guy.

She told her mother that she had to go back to the employment office the following Friday but instead she found her way back to *"Frankie Joy."* They had sex several times before he decided to elope with her.

He took her to various states and the purpose was prostitution. He had her peddling her body all over the country, while her parents were in hot pursuit.

He was changing states so often it was very difficult to pin them down.

Her mother got a wire that they were seen in California so she sold her house and moved to California. By then, they had left California and went to New York where poor Jennifer became pregnant again.

It was ten long years before he brought Jennifer back to Chicago. The culprit had married her for prostitution purposes and the law could not touch him. He had dogged her terribly, treated her like some animal that had been thrown in the garbage.

When he moved back to Chicago, out of pity, his brother gave them a place to live. Jennifer had grown to a certain stage; she was now 29 years old and wanted to contact her mother to tell her that she was married and had another child.

She had to go and serve as a prostitute on the north-side of Chicago each and every night; regardless of the weather - it could be -20 degrees below zero but she had to go and could not return unless she had made her quota of $200 a night.

When her mother saw Jennifer's condition, she threatened to take her home. The culprit got vicious and cussed the mother out shoving her out of the house and ended up throwing bricks at her.

The police were called but the culprit had the upper hand as far as the law was concerned. After the mother left, he beat Jennifer for getting in touch with her mother. After that, Jennifer had to really work — sometimes she tried to rebel because of the weather. She didn't have boots, gloves, scarves, etc., but he always threatened to put her out if she didn't go.

Jennifer had forsaken her mother for her so-called husband and thought she was doomed. His brother was a prominent attorney and only tolerated him because of brotherhood.

Soon Jennifer was pregnant again but by one of her street dates. He put her and the baby on welfare and he got on general assistance. Even during her months of pregnancy, he would not let it interfere with her going to get him money. Right up until the time her water bag broke, she had to keep performing prostitution acts.

Jennifer had the baby but before her six-weeks checkup, she was back on the streets turning tricks. She tried to explain to him that she was in no condition to deal with the streets but he threatened to kick her out of the house. It was one of the saddest situations on earth.

All the money went toward his habit of free-basing cocaine. Every night, she must bring in at least $200. Her welfare check, his general assistance check all went toward cocaine. He took her for granted and thought like all the other fools —that this would last forever. He refused to let her spend a dime of the money on her children or herself, everything went for the cocaine pipe.

Eventually God stepped in and dealt the fatal blow. Jennifer saw how he watched over the newborn baby and her motherly instincts surfaced. One night he sent her out to work and she came back very late. She had drunk too much and he had warned her to never drink; especially while trying to get his cocaine money together.

For the first time ever, she came prepared for a full-blown confrontation with him. He had never seen her in this state of mind.

"Here punk", she told him as she tossed $30 on the bed. "You are no pimp, you are a *simp*. Any other man would treat me better than you. If it wasn't for me and your brother, you'd starve to death. *I've given you nearly $1 million since I've known you and all you can find to do with it is smoke it up!*

The $30 is a baby-sitting fee and you are not even a good baby-sitter.   I'm taking my baby and leaving," she firmly announced.

He got up and beat poor Jennifer with an iron pipe and threw her out. She went to her mother's house for the first time in twelve (12) years. She and her mother called the police; who took her over to the house to pick the children up. Frankie Joy was arrested for battery, but his brother, the lawyer, pulled a few strings and got him out in a flash. But he was never to see Jennifer again.

His cocaine supply had been cut off entirely. His meal ticket, his means of survival, Jennifer, was gone. He had mental lapses and eventually snapped completely. He started throwing bricks at all his friends houses where he thought Jennifer might be hiding.

While on one of these throwing sprees, he struck a man with one of the bricks and broke his arm. He went on to threaten to kill some people, saying that they were instrumental in Jennifer's leaving. He continued to throw rocks and bricks at people's homes until one man took a shot at him and that is what slowed him down.

The last time he was ever seen or heard from, the bum was standing around a 10 gallon drum can with several other homeless, trying to keep warm during the bitter cold months.

Frankie Joy never regretted the way he had *"handled Jennifer."* That's the sad part. He would go through the rest of his miserable life taking all his actions out on others and never realizing who the real fool was.

3. HYPOCRITE PIMP

"Oscar, I've opened up a clothing store and I need your help. You're living with your brother and his wife but you also know that you are not wanted. Why don't you come with me? I'll pay you a small salary. In exchange you can keep the store clean and learn the sales techniques. There is also a nice room in the back of the store that you can have rent free," Rudy told Oscar.

"How soon can I start?" asked Oscar, with a cunning snake-like smile.

Rudy had been somewhat of a friend to Oscar even though everybody else knew him to be a left-handed villain. Oscar was the sinister type. The kind the movies portray as the lowest type of villain.

Rudy hired Oscar as a handyman at the store. Oscars's job was washing the windows, mopping the floors, and taking out the trash. He was doing a fairly decent job as the weeks rolled into months and he became known around as the *"guy who slept in the back of Rudy's clothing store."*

A lady, by the name of Helen, who had a romantic interest in Rudy stopped in the store to chat one day and after a lengthy conversation with her about what a low-down rotten and wrong fellow Rudy was, which was a lie, Oscar had practically convinced her that all the above were true about Rudy and naturally her feelings started to wane.

Rudy could not understand the silent treatment he was receiving from Helen and one day decided to call her to ask what was the problem.

"I heard that you were a pimp in disguise, - a **Hypocrite Pimp**. All you want is to use my money in your enterprises and then find an excuse to drop me," she told him.

"Where could you possibly have heard something as ridiculous as that!" Rudy exclaimed.

"I am a businessman," he pleaded.

"Never mind who or what my source is; you just forget my phone number," she angrily told Rudy.

At Oscar's urging, she started having cocktails and dinner with him. She was a professional woman, a registered nurse with the federal government and owned her home in the suburbs. One night while they were out, Oscar slipped a *"mickey"* in her drink. He already knew that she lived alone and when she got drowsy, he suggested that he should drive her home and she consented. When they arrived at her house, she was completely out. Once they were inside, he applied cold towels to her forehead, under the pretense of sobering her up, undressed her and put her to bed. He hurriedly undressed, got in bed with her and took full sexual advantage of her all night.

The next morning when she came around he laid beside her pretending to be asleep.

"Hey, what are you doing here?" she cried in astonishment. "Why baby you took sick, maybe you had too much to drink, so I drove you home; you insisted that I did not leave you alone. I tried to leave but you begged me not to go," he lied.

"What time is it?" She asked and shook her head as if to get the cobwebs out.

Oscar looked at the clock.

"It's 10:45 in the morning," he told her.

"Oh, I am so ashamed of myself. I've never done anything like this in my life before," she told him.

"Did we have sex last night?" she asked in amazement.

"Several times, baby, several times," he proudly told her.   "Wow. I must have really been out of it; I am very particular about who I sleep with," she said.

"You insisted baby, you insisted," he lied again.

"I did?" she asked with open eyes of disbelief.

"And I was high myself or I might have turned you down," he said, telling another lie.

"Well, it's too late to go to work so I'll call in and we can finish where we left off," she said.

Oscar winked at the wall and said to himself, *"I have struck it again."*

She made her call and fell back into Oscar's frail arms and the love session was on.

Oscar played the handyman for Rudy at the store but didn't let an opportunity pass where he steadily preached to her of his dislike for Rudy because of him being a pimp.

"If a woman did me a favor, I'd be eternally grateful and repay her as soon as possible but I just can't stand a pimp," he lied.

He finally persuaded her to take sides against Rudy with him.

"You could live here with me, if you'd like; I'll help you find a job. I like you Oscar, you don't have to sleep in the back of Rudy's store any more."

Oscar took her up on it and moved in bag and baggage. She proved to be extremely generous to Oscar. While she worked, Oscar stayed home. Whenever he hung out with his no good buddies, he would lie to her and pretend he had been job hunting. Oscar had a friend named Charles, who he greatly admired as a pimp, at the same time, he was very jealous of Charles.

Charles knew of Oscar's low-life traits, would feed him, but with a long-handled spoon. Oscar could not help brag about taking Rudy's woman and how Rudy was a fool for blowing such a good woman, and how he had been stealing money from the clothing store.

Charles smiled slightly but didn't appreciate it one bit.

Oscar came up with the idea to buy a car for which he had no cash. Helen gave him $1,000 to buy a car but he needed $1,500 so he borrowed $500 from his pimp friend, Charles. When he bought the Ford (Charles only drove Cadillacs), Oscar thought he was the *"cat's meow"* or the *"dog's bow-wow."*

To wallow in his good-times, Oscar started seeking out Rudy to show off just how well he was doing. He stepped out of his Ford as though it was a Rolls Royce and he was King Farouk.

Finally, one day he was telling Rudy, "See man, you never carry a sign on your back saying I'm a pimp; you have to ease up on the broads and by the time they wake up, they've been pimped on and pimped on good. You know that broad that used to come by to see you, she saw me out one night and told me she had gotten over you and wanted me to be her man. I know you would rather I pimp on her than some stranger," he told Rudy as he gave him a ride around the block in his new Ford.

"Well, Oscar, you both have my blessings and I wish you all the best of luck," Rudy told him.

A week later, Oscar drove by Rudy's store and Rudy was gone but his wife was there. It was closing time and Oscar offered to drop her off at home saying, "I could use the cab fare," with a sneaky grin. She accepted the ride.

While on the way to her house, Oscar clear out of the blue started telling her about affairs that Rudy had been having with other women.

"Where's Rudy now? I bet you don't know," he told her.

"He just told me to watch the store while he took care of some important business," she told him.

"He told me that if he was late to just close the store and catch a cab home. Rudy has no reason to have to deal with other women. I am a faithful, good wife to him and good mother to the girls," she explained.

"Well, it always has been a mystery to me why a beautiful girl like you would stay with a guy like Rudy. You are pretty and young, I just can't understand some women," he rambled on.

"I guess you have to be a woman to understand," she tearfully said, as she dropped her head.

"You can do a lot better than that, I could take you where he is right now. He's making a fool of you and as a matter of fact, he's over at Cheri's house right now," he told her.

"Who's Cheri?" she inquired as she looked up at Oscar as he slowly drove her home.

"That's his other woman. He does as much for her as he does for you and your children," Oscar retorted.

"Where does she live?" she asked.

"I will pass by her house and I bet you will see Rudy's car parked in the driveway," he told her.

Oscar had always been jealous of the way women were attracted to Rudy, especially Cheri, he had always wanted her. "He pays her bills and just bought her a floor model TV," he added.

Oscar drove past Cheri's house and surely, there was Rudy's car parked in the driveway.

"Now you see with your own eyes, but don't you ever let him know I did this favor for you, you see, I like you myself," he told her.

Rudy's marriage went on the rocks, followed by a divorce. Rudy lost the clothing store and relocated to California.

Oscar and Charles really became running partners. Charles went into real estate and opened an office on a business street and Oscar was something like a runner, just to be in Charles' company.

He made it possible for Oscar to make a nice buck, after he had legally married his main girl who had helped him to get setup in business.

Oscar was his main man. Oscar was flying high. He was on cloud nine. He and Charles had plenty of women, fun time together, and Oscar knew all of his business as far as other women were concerned. The real estate office turned into a haven after hours. Women, women, and more women; Oscar was living first class.

Charles had a beautiful Creole prostitute, Rosetta, who was bringing him money by the pounds from downtown. You only had to notice the nervous tick, the gleam in his eye, and stammering when he spoke, to realize that Oscar had secretly fallen in love with her.

Charles realized just how badly other men wanted her and being a pimp, he was always able to come up with an outstanding idea. He and his little peach came up with the idea to pretend that they had broken up, after she had explained to him how many big time fellows had been trying to offer her money. Charles started sending her in on guys with the bucks and it was paying off. Oscar's jealousy began to swell.

Glasses, a big time dope man, wanted some part of this little peach in the worst way. Charles cut the strings and told her to go after him. She made herself noticeable to Glasses and when Glasses hit on her, she told him that Charles was no longer her man because she had asked him to buy her a car and pay off a bond she had jumped but he had refused.

"Baby, if you be my woman, I'd buy the car, pay off the bond, and get whatever else you wanted," he bragged.

"Would you Glasses?" she coyly asked.

"Just say you are mine," he said with his huge stomach hanging over his belt.

"I'm yours then, Glasses," she announced.

Glasses gave her $1,800 to take care of her business with a promise of more later. She spent the night with Glasses and the next morning she gave the $1,800 to Charles.

That evening, Charles was kidding with Oscar when he came by the office.

"See boy, this is the way the pimp game goes," he said while flashing eighteen, $100 bills. Oscar's eyes almost popped out of their sockets.

Later that night, Oscar saw the little peach in the car with Glasses. He couldn't wait to get back to Charles with the news. "Look Charles, you know that I love you like a brother; now don't go getting yourself in trouble about a broad, but I just saw your little piece in the car with that big shot dope, Glasses. She didn't see me but that's the way of a woman," he told Charles.

"Thanks Oscar, but no thanks. Do me a favor, if you happen to see one of my women with a bear, please don't tell me," Charles told him.

"Well man, I just didn't want you to get yourself in trouble over a female and that guy is a heavy."

"Oscar, I am not a hypocrite pimp; I am a pimp and don't care who knows it because you can't pimp a successful lie. I'm not trying to play the game and escape the name. Any woman who chooses me knows what to expect. The one who does the choosing, does the paying," Charles explained to Oscar.

That night, Rosetta called Charles with $1,300 more and told him how much she loved him and that he didn't have to worry about Glasses, he was nothing but a big fat slob and is about oral sex only.

Oscar saw her again riding around with Glasses, having big fun spending money with his window dressing. The little peach would make anybody look good and the way she carried on over Glasses really fascinated him.

When Oscar saw Charles at the office the next morning, the little peach was there. She kissed Charles and left.

"Man what is that little broad trying to pull? Last night I saw her and Glasses again and now I see her with you; what's her story?" Oscar frowned as he spoke.

"Oscar, you are my man, but you've got the wrong idea about how the pimp game goes. It's a love game. Like I told you, I'm not trying to play this game and escape the name. See you don't want to be called a pimp but you want what a pimp is supposed to get. Any of my women can go when they get ready and come back when they please, because I'm going to charge them for it any way," Charles told Oscar as he counted out thirteen more $100 dollar bills.

"Glasses was paying off wonderfully." Oscar's eyes glared with jealousy. He tried to smile but any one could tell he was faking.

Now, coincidentally, Oscar had gone to school with Glasses' main woman. He grabbed his hat and went straight to her brother's house and got her address.

He noticed that Glasses' car was not there so he rang the doorbell.

She looked through a peep hole and asked, "Who is it?"

"Oscar, Oscar James," he hollered through the door.

"Oh hello, Oscar, boy I haven't seen you for ages. Where have you been and what storm blew you this way?" she smiled as she opened the door to a man-sion-like home.

Oscar went in, she took his hat and offered him a seat and a drink.

"Well, I just saw Harold , your brother, and he told me where you were living; I didn't know Glasses was your husband," he stated.

"Well, we are not legally married but we have been together so long he's the only man that I will ever be satisfied with. He is so good to me," she said.

"Well, I like you as a friend and I hate to see things going down to people that I care about. It's just not right."

"I don't understand what you're getting at," she said.

"You see Margaret, you said you had a man but what you have is a trick. He's buying new cars and giving away a lot of money to one of my friend's woman, a little Creole girl. She's cleaning him out. You can catch them any night at Lovie's lounge," he told her.

"Well thanks a lot Oscar, I figured something was wrong; he has been acting a bit strange lately."

Their talk continued until Oscar decided that he had talked enough; she saw him to the door and waved him good-by.

The next morning, Glasses pulled up in front of Charles' real estate office. He got out of his car and went in.

"Hey Charles, it's Glasses, I'd like to have a little talk with you," he said.

"Yeah man, come on in the back office," Charles waved. "This little girl that you use to have, Rosetta, told me that you and her had broken up and I just want to know something. I gave her $1,300 night before last and she can't account for any of it. Are you two playing a *game* on me? My wife said somebody stopped by the house and told her he saw you with the $1,300. I don't want any trouble man, you just give me my money back and take your girl," Glasses said.

"Hey man, I have two or three women that give me money, and a lot of people might have seen me with more than $1,300. I'm in business; I didn't even know you knew Rosetta. So since you got her you keep her because I don't want or need her," Charles lied.

Glasses stormed out of the door, "Well man, I'm telling you, I just don't want no shit," and he slammed the door and left.

As soon as he was gone, Charles realized who the informer was. He had only shown the money to one person —Oscar.

Charles began to wonder just what kind of fellow Oscar really was. He had been very nice to him; loaned him money to help get his Ford; let him make money from his business, and even gave him money at times. What kind of guy would do such a thing?

But Charles didn't want to beat up on a coward. There are more than one ways to skin a cat. Charles began setting traps for Oscar.

Glasses roughed the little girl Rosetta up and she left and went back to New Orleans but she didn't forget to send Charles some money; she was in love with him.

When Oscar came by the office a couple of mornings later, Charles decided not to mention anything.

"Hey Oscar, old buddy," he said in a gleeful manner.   "Oscar, you know people are beginning to rate you with me but I can't have a partner riding around in a cheap Ford. I hate to say it man but if you can't come up with a Cadillac, I'm afraid I'm going to have to cut you loose. Tell that woman of yours that you've got to get a different ride."

"Yeah, yeah. I think she'll get me one," he sheepishly said.

When Oscar got home that night he started talking Cadillac talk. She balked at it so he stole her jewelry and mink coats and got enough to pay down on a pretty white Cadillac, which immediately made him *"the lion's road."*

His woman called the police after she discovered the theft and had him thrown out of her house, so he went to his brother's house.

Charles got high and hid some money in the base of the telephone, six hundred dollars($600). When Charles looked for the money, it was gone. Oscar was the only person who knew where the money was hidden. However, when he questioned Oscar, of course, Oscar denied it, so Charles gave him another pass.

Charles had set up all these traps for Oscar, waiting for the finale. When Oscar finally eased around and told Charles' wife a bunch of lies about what he had been doing with women and money, that was the straw that broke the camel's back.

It was a rainy Wednesday morning, about 9:00 a.m., when Oscar showed up at Charles' office. He came in grinning. Charles spoke as if nothing was wrong and waited until Oscar had taken a seat, then he went to his coat, took out a .38 snub nose. He walked over to Oscar and hit him up side the head with the pistol and blood flew all over the place.

Then he knocked Oscar to the floor and started kicking him as he called him foul names. He beat him to a pulp while Oscar tried to crawl to the door to escape but Charles was constantly pistol whipping him. Oscar tried to run but Charles grabbed his coat as, he tried to flee. He was continually popping him up side the head with the pistol and kicking him in the rear end. Oscar managed somehow to come out of the coat and got away. But not before Charles had nearly beaten him to death.

The months passed and Oscar got delinquent with his car payments and was ducking the financiers. One night he went out to the airport and when he returned to where he had parked, the car was gone.

Oscar fell back to where he belonged, deep in the bowels of the ghetto and was never heard from again. Although it was rumored he traveled to California in search of Rudy.

4. DOPE-FIEND PIMP

Sharon was a beautiful young woman, just 19 years of age. She was as fresh and lovely as the first rose in May. She came from an affluent background and was a sophomore in college. Her parents resided in Olympia Fields, a suburb of Chicago.

Considered high middle-class, she was musically inclined and a jazz fanatic. Ninety-five percent of her associates were musicians. She would always show up wherever there was a jazz set or jam session.

With her light complexion, black shoulder-length hair and keen features, she was often mistaken for a Caucasian. With her body, she could easily become an understudy for Sophia Loren.

Very few normal men could pass her without taking a second glance. Soon the fast crowd began to take notice of her. The pimps craved for her attention because they realized that their money would grow from the floor to the ceiling if they were lucky enough to catch her. But if one wasn't about music, they didn't stand a possible chance.

Again the devil rose his ugly head. There was a dope fiend pimp who could have passed as her twin brother; a very handsome hunk. He had to have her regardless of the circumstances and also realizing that with her his $100 a day dope habit would be very easy to afford.

He made special arrangements to go to several rummage outlets to purchase a secondhand trombone and case.

He stalked Sharon like a wild animal would stalk his prey. One Friday night at the Strand Lounge in Chicago, a big jazz extravaganza was appearing, the cocktail lounge was overflowing with jazz fans and Sharon was one of them. Aaron, the dope-fiend admirer had his woman, Sarah, who was also an addict, well schooled as to how to go about making friends with Sharon in order to rope and hog tie her.

Aaron and Sarah resided at the old Evans Hotel at 43rd Street and Drexel, which was considered upper-class at the time with its swank apartments with cooking facilities.

Sarah was to befriend Sharon by telling her that her husband was a musician and was to play on the set. Sharon was known to be star struck by any aspiring musician. Aaron and Sarah donned their best attire. With his trombone in hand, they headed to the jam session.

They took a booth next to the one that Sharon and two other jazz fanatics occupied. Aaron sat calmly with his trombone case across his lap while he clapped openly, keeping time with the beat of the music.

Sharon glanced his way but he pretended he didn't see her. Sarah was making her rounds from table to table smiling, shaking hands and making small talk with everyone she thought she knew, while working her way to Sharon's booth, which was adjacent to theirs.

It didn't take long before she had reached her destination. "Hi, my name is Sarah," she said to the three girls who occupied the booth next to the one she and Aaron had.

"I'm Louise."

"I'm Thelma."

"I'm Sharon." The three girls introduced themselves.

"My husband is playing on the set tonight, he's a trombonist." Sarah focused her attention on Sharon.

"I don't think I know your husband, who is he?" Sharon spoke up.

"Aaron Anderson, you never heard of him honey,

but he's the best," Sarah boasted with a joking smile.

"No, I've never heard of him, have you two heard of him?" Sharon turned to the two girls who were sitting with her.

"No, I haven't."

"Me either," the other girls said.

"Well, let me introduce you all," Sarah said as she called Aaron over and introduced him to the three girls.

The boys on the stand were blowing away and the crowd was really enjoying it. One of the girls at the table was greeted by an old musician; he called her from the booth and took her to the bar.

Aaron made conversation with the other girl while Sarah talked to Sharon.

"Sharon, could you excuse yourself for a minute? Come and go to the ladies room with me." Sharon agreeably went to the ladies room with Sarah.

"I've been noticing you, at most of the jazz sets. I'm a music lover too, not just any kind of music, jazz is my favorite," Sarah told her.

"Yes, I just love it; it's my life and livelihood," Sharon said.

"You said that you have never seen or heard my husband play, well he's one step from being rated tops in the music polls and he's playing with Dexter Gordon on the 23rd of May. That's next month and I will tell you what I'm going to do, I'm going to give you and your friends a few free tickets to the show," Sarah told her.

"Oh, would you really be that kind," Sharon's eyes lit up. "Of course, I would," Sarah told her. "It will be at the Savoy and we can go together. That way you can get a chance to meet Dexter and some of the other greats. I know you would enjoy the show if you are a true jazz fan," Sarah told her.

They swapped telephone numbers and went

back to their seats to finish listening to the boys play. The night ended and the time had run out for Aaron to get a chance to blow his trombone. Sharon regretted not being able to hear Aaron play but Sarah explained that time had run out.

Back at the hotel preparing to take a fix, Aaron told Sarah, "You are my baby, Sarah. You did just fine with that chick... do you think you can pull it off?"

"No problem baby, no problem. She's naive and weak as water," Sharon said.

"Did she go for me being a musician?" Aaron asked.

"She went for everything. I told her I wanted her to go to the Savoy with me next month so she could hear you play and that she would have the opportunity to meet more music giants. You should have seen how she lit up. We'll have her strung out by then," Sarah told her man.

Aaron was nodding but he raised his head long enough to chuckle and mumbled out, "Fine, baby, just fine."

The next day, Sharon kept her promise and called Sarah and the girls talked for a long time as the experienced dope-fiend prostitute lied to the inexperienced and naive Sharon.

Aaron sat on the side of the bed, nodding in agreement to what Sarah was telling Sharon.

Sharon was invited over to dinner the following Sunday. Thinking that a music celebrity was to be present, she accepted the invitation.

"What does it look like?" Aaron asked.

"Well she is a sophomore in college. She lives in Olympia Fields. Her mother is Black, her father is Jewish. She doesn't go steady with anyone. She has only had sex three times and those were not about money. She said her favorite soul dinners are macaroni and cheese, string beans and corn bread. Ha, ha, ha, that's the Black side in her," Sarah said.

"That's good baby. That's good. Now we are going to show that little fine bitch something that she will
never forget. We'll give her some green beans alright.
Now, this is what I want you to do. Buy three cans of
string beans, open them and set them in the laundry
room where no one will find them; let them remain
there until next Sunday. They'll be spoiled rotten. I'll
get some knockout drops from Doc Gray and spice it in
the macaroni and cheese. Just tell old Doc that he can
have sex with this fine young bitch and he'll be glad to
accommodate. You got it?" lectured Aaron.

"Yes, daddy I got you."

Aaron was Sarah's God almighty. She was black
as night and Aaron's slave.

Aaron called Doc Gray and told him the whole
deal. They had done this type of thing several times
before. It was nothing new to Aaron or the Doc. Doc
Gray was also invited to dinner but was forewarned as
to what foods to eat.

When the moment of truth arrived, Sharon, sur-
prisingly showed first, then the Doc. Sarah started
bringing dinner to the table while Doc prepared a drink
for himself, Sharon and Aaron.

Sharon asked to help with the dinner but was
told that she was a guest. As they gathered around the
table, talking about different types of musicians, Sharon
was extremely excited.

Sarah served roast beef, spinach, mashed pota-
toes, macaroni and cheese (spiked), string beans
(spiked), and Sharon showed her appreciation by really enjoying the macaroni and cheese and string beans.

She bragged about the taste of everything and
said that she wished she could cook as good as Sarah.

After dinner, the wine flowed. That was all
Sharon drank and now was the time for old Doc to ad-
minister the knockout drops. They gave Sarah the sig-

nal to pull Sharon in the bedroom for a while; just long enough for them to load her drink.

"Sharon, come here a minute honey. There's a little woman talk that the men aren't suppose to hear," Sarah beckoned Sharon.

When Sharon went in the bedroom, Sarah went to her closet and brought out some marijuana, "Do you smoke weed?" Sarah asked.   "No, I never have but I don't have any objection to what other people do unless they are dope addicts. I don't associate with dope addicts," Sharon said.

Sarah kept her in the room ample time and then called out, "Would one of you gentlemen be nice enough to bring our drinks to the room?" The Doc had really taken care of his part of the deal. He rushed to the room with the girls' drinks on a tray.

Sharon was busting with laughter and really enjoying her self. As the chatter lingered on, Sarah kept saying "I wonder what happened to the boys. We intended to surprise you Sharon with a little music but it looks like the boys have let us down."

About 30 minutes later, Sharon told Sarah to show her to the bathroom. She held her stomach as Sarah showed her the way to the bathroom. Sarah, Doc and Aaron all looked at each other.

When Sharon got to the bathroom, she vomited string beans and macaroni and cheese all over the floor, stool and sink.

"Oh, I feel terrible; I'm sick, I guess I must have eaten too much," she said to Sarah as she came into the bathroom. "Here baby, let me help you."

"You must have enjoyed Sarah's cooking too much," the Doc said as he searched his black medical bag.

They placed Sharon on the bed and the Doc gave her a pill and soon she was fast asleep. Sarah removed her clothing and crawled in the bed with her. She cradled Sharon in her arms like a baby and started talking motherly talk to her. Aaron closed the door.

Soon sounds came from the room as if a male and female were having sex but it was Sarah having oral sex with Sharon, getting her ready for Doc.

Even though Sharon was drugged, she tried to push Sarah's head away but she semi-enjoyed it and moaned and other times groaned. Soon, she held Sarah's head tightly, widened her legs and just fell back and relaxed.

Sarah came out of the room and told Doc, "There she is Doc, all yours."

About an hour later, the Doc came out of the room grinning and zipping up his fly.

Aaron then went to the room and that's where he remained until late that night. Sharon began to stir and raised up and looked around.

"Oh, my stomach. Where am I?"

"You are in safe hands, baby. You are with Aaron. Hey, Doc, come here," Aaron called through the door.

When the Doc came in the room, Aaron told him her stomach was still bothering her and asked him if he had anything else he could give her.

The Doc left the room and loaded a hypodermic needle with morphine... "This will not hurt you but will make you relax," the Doc told her as he injected the needle in her arm.

She quickly fell back to sleep. All three of them made love to her again while she was unconscious. The Doc had to leave because it was getting late but he left enough knockout drops and other forms of drugs with Aaron and Sarah to keep her cool until he could return.

Whenever Aaron and Sarah would shoot up and Sharon would groggily awake, they would always shoot her up with morphine while they used heroin.

For the next three days, Sharon had found a new home. The Doc would come and go, enjoying his sexual pleasures with Sharon and would always leave a certain amount of morphine.

After so many days, the free morphine ran out and Sharon had a terrible craving for it. She begged without shame for it only to be told that it was very expensive and that they had run out of money but told her that the Doc liked her and she could make a deal with him to get her some and they explained what the deal was.

Sharon understood and agreed. She didn't want to go home. She didn't want any food or music. She didn't want to go to school. All she wanted was a fix.

They realized they had scored and now it was time to go to work.

"Bitch, we have spent a lot of money on you. That shit that you say makes you feel good is not free. It don't come free, whore. It costs money. You got to get off your lazy ass and do something to get some money," Aaron pimped.

Sarah voiced, "Yeah, Sharon, he's right; we've spent a nice buck on you. If you want, you can come with me and we can make some money."

"I'll do anything, just get me another fix," Sharon begged. "Ok, I'll get you another fix, but you'll have to get your ass out of here tonight and you had better have some goddamn money," Aaron growled.

There were so many men who had been waiting for a long time to have sex with the beautiful Sharon that it was no problem at all for her to take her pick. She was a hot commodity. She made plenty money for Aaron and Sarah the first night out.

For months her parents listed her with the Missing Persons Bureau but Sharon didn't want to go to her parents. Her home was now with Aaron and Sarah. They placed her in a downtown upper-class hotel where she would bring home $1,000 to $1,200 every Tuesday. That type of hotel would not accept a woman of Sarah's complexion but she would take Sharon a fix every so often.

Three months passed and the hotel got hot and Sharon had to hit the streets again but she still made good money. Six months passed and she was finally picked up by the vice squad for prostitution. She then decided to call her parents and headed back home to her family. But the craving of the mighty morphine rose its ugly head. She stole $600 from her parents and headed back to Aaron and Sarah.

A year later, Sharon was the biggest tramp on 63rd Street.   The corner of 63rd and Cottage Grove was her stomping ground. If you look closely today, you might just see an old gray headed, bent over "White" lady still trying to catch a trick.

5. THE BLACKMAIL PIMP

"Hello, pretty girl. Give me a package of spearmint gum and a carton of Kool cigarettes," the handsome young man said to the very attractive young sales clerk at the corner drug store.

She gave him the gum and cigarettes. He gave her a fifty dollar bill to impress her.

"Have you ever tried modeling? You are an awfully pretty girl," he told her.

"No, I don't think my husband would like that," she smiled.   Peggy was a tall, leggy girl, slightly knock-kneed, this only added to her striking good looks. She had dyed her hair an eye-catching auburn color, which matched her smooth complexion.

Roger had seen something of value and he had to get her, regardless of the consequences. He made it his business to go by every day and flirt with her but she only told him that she was true blue to her husband. That still did not deter Roger's intentions one way or the other.

Peggy got to know Roger pretty well by his coming in the store but not well enough to cheat on her husband, who was there every night to pick her up from work.

Roger thought and schemed in every way that he knew, on how to get her to go out with him but nothing worked. Roger lived alone in an apartment in Hyde Park and had to figure some way to get this peach the way he had gotten so many before her - husband or no husband.

As the weeks turned into months, Peggy and Roger became chummier and chummier but still not enough for her to cheat on her husband. Peggy was a very naive young woman. Her husband had been her only man. He had married her when she became pregnant at age 16 and now she was twenty-three and knew nothing of the world, nor the people in it.

Roger went to the camera shop and brought himself a camera that could take pictures in the dark without a flash. He paid a carpenter to install it facing his bed and put the switch at the head of it. He practiced daily, perfecting his knowledge of the camera.

He knew that he would eventually wear her resistance down but as time went by, it seemed as though she was never going to make the fatal mistake of getting involved with Roger.

But as fate would have it, one day Roger was downtown shopping, loaded with packages and decided to have a little lunch. As he entered Ted's Steak House and stood in line to order, Peggy walked in. She didn't see Roger.

He got his food and headed to the upper floor. She headed downstairs, that's when he noticed her.

"Peggy," he shouted and jumped up from the table. He took her tray and said, "Come join me at my table or I'll join you at yours."

"Roger, what a surprise, what are you doing downtown? I thought you never left that corner." She was delighted. She trailed him to the upper floor.

As they sat, ate and talked, she wondered whether or not she was doing the right thing. But what could it hurt, after all she was in a public place.

"Oh, I've been doing a little shopping," he told her.

"So you're spending a lot of money, huh? Some have it, some don't," she said as she cut her steak.

"Had I known I would have seen you, I'd have brought you a present. You don't have to tell your husband everything because he's not going to tell you everything he does," he told her.

"Oh yes he does. He is very faithful," she said. That's how naive she was.

He took out a big roll of money, quite obviously for her benefit.

"Roger, where do you get so much money? Me and my husband together don't handle the kind of money you just seem to throw away."

"You both don't do anything to get any money. You ever heard of anybody getting rich from a job? Pretty as you are, you could have anything you want but you are just like all the rest, let a fool lock you up while you are young until your youth goes and then he's gone too," he pimped.

"Sometimes I think people like you are better off than working folks like me, but I don't know anything else to do. I wouldn't dare sell my body."

"But I bet you'd give some away. Which is the smartest, to sell it or give it away?" he pimped.

"I like you Peggy and I want to do something

nice for you. What did you come downtown for?"

"I came down here to buy me a dress. I am almost out of clothes."

"What dress size and pants size do you wear? I sell women's clothes." he told her.

"A size 10 dress and size 12 pants," she answered.

"Save your money. I've got something I will give you with no strings attached but you will have to go to my apartment to get them."

"I don't go to men's apartments Roger."

But when Roger was finished talking to her, she was in his car and on her way to his apartment.

They finally reached Roger's specially laid out pad; carpeted throughout, bar combined with a record player, stocked with all types of wines and other spirits.

His sofa was purple velvet and the color TV was in the place where a fireplace once was. He had a king size bed with mirrored walls and ceiling, to be able to watch all bed action.

"Roger this is beautiful. This is some layout. Why don't you have a wife. I wish I had an apartment like this. Gee, this is really something," she marveled.

"Well baby, I am not looking for a headache and wives are headaches. They expect to sit on their asses and the husbands do all the bread winning. I was married once, but she divorced me while I was in jail. Would you like a drink?"

"I don't really drink but I'll take a white wine to be sociable," she smiled.

Roger reached in his clothes closet and brought out some choice women pieces. Leather and knit, suede and leather, etc.. Most of them were her size.

"Here, go in the bathroom and try these on."

"Hey, Peggy, I just learned how to make a martini. I want you to taste one with me. Niggers don't drink martinis," he grinned.

She came out of the bathroom wearing one of the dresses and looking spectacular.

"How do I look?" she asked, turning round and round.

"Just fabulous baby. It doesn't take much for you to look good any way."

Roger was making the martinis and he made hers very mild, with a semi-sweet taste. "Here, taste this."

She approached it as if it was fire.

"It won't hurt you. Go ahead and taste it. Here, let me taste it first." He took a sip then passed it back to her.

"So this is what they call a martini, huh?" She smacked her lips.

"How does it taste?"

"It's nice, tastes a little sweet."

When she went back to the bathroom to finish trying on the outfits, he poured a bit more gin in her martini and turned on his camera gimmick.
She sipped on the martini. He offered her cocaine and reefer but she hastily refused both.

But when she had finished her first martini, she asked if she could have another and that's when the thing went down.

He gave her a *mickey* and it wasn't long before she fell across his bed and he was busy kissing her. It didn't take long before she was helpless and he removed her clothes.

First he took pictures of her in the nude. Then he placed his penis in her mouth and took some. Next, he put her in the buck with those long legs resting on his arms as he lay between them on his knees. He took as many different poses as he could and then made love to her for a long time. Occasionally, she would respond by calling out her husband's name -"*Oh, Eddie*" or an occasional moan. He got on the phone and called a bunch of his *"no-pussy-getting"* buddies and they had sex with her as Roger snapped pictures.

The party was finally over and all the fellows were gone. He tried to wake her as it had gotten quite late but was unsuccessful. When she finally did wake up, it was 2:30 a.m.

"Oh my God, where am I? What the hell, where am I?"

Roger pretended to be asleep. He was lying next to her in the nude too.

"Oh my God, what can I do, please help me Roger. I didn't pick my little boy up from school and what time is it?" She was in a complete shock.

"Huh baby, what's the matter?" Roger was acting as though he had just woke up. He tried to kiss her but she jerked her head away.

"What's the matter baby? A while ago you told me you were mine and you didn't want to go home anymore. Now you don't even want to kiss me. What's wrong?"

"I did not say that," she frowned.

"Ah baby, don't play dumb. You told me if I didn't find you a lot of dick that you would go back home. So I called some of my pals over and you had a lot of fun.

"I did what?" She grabbed the phone and called her mother. "Mama, has Eddie called your house?"

"Yes. Where in the world have you been girl? Everybody is worried sick about you," her mother told her.

"I'm over at Carrie's house but mama I had too much to drink and fell asleep. What did Eddie say?"

"Well, he said he had to pick the baby up from school when he got home because the teacher called him and he was very upset," her mother told her.

When she hung up the telephone, Roger told her, "Baby, you might as well rest because you belong to me now."

"Oh no, I've got to be getting home. If I don't, I'm in big trouble."

"You don't know how much trouble you are in if you try and go," he told her.

"What do you mean?" She asked him.

"I mean that you are my woman. That's what I mean bitch."

"Bitch, who are you calling a bitch?" She rebelled.

"You, bitch, you that's who," he shouted. He got out of bed and went to the drawer and got ten or twelve different poses he had shot of her. One was with her vagina wide open and various others that she would rather die than have anyone see of her, she almost fainted.

"Oh my God! No, no, no, please tear them up. I'll do anything you want me to. If you would just tear them up. Please Roger, come on and make love to me. Do anything you want but just tear those filthy pictures up."

Roger's scheme had worked perfectly. He laid back and gave himself credit for being so shrewd.

"Well baby, since you have been gone this long, you might as well make a night of it. We'll think of something in the morning. How much money do you and your husband have saved?" He asked as he rubbed her hot spot an kissed her like he had always wanted.

"About three thousand dollars. We are trying to buy a house but you can have the money. Just please give me those pictures," she pleaded.

"I'll tell you what, he said, what day of the week is this?"

"Friday," she said.

"When can you get the money out of the bank?"

"Well, they are closed tomorrow, can you wait until Monday?" she asked him.

"Look baby, I have to have about five grand."

"But we only have three and that's all we have in the world. I don't know where we would get anymore."

He replied, "I do. Hell, you laid up here and fucked and sucked all those niggers. Just giving it away. What's wrong with selling some?"

"I don't know what came over me to do such a thing but pictures don't lie," she said sadly.

"You have really messed things up so you might as well make the best of it. You see, I want you to be my woman and before I see you go, I'll send the goddam pictures to everybody that knows you," he threatened.

He kept pouring alcohol into her, and making love to her from Friday to Monday. On Monday he drove her by her house to get the bank book to withdraw the three thousand dollars from the bank.

After returning to his house with the money, he made a telephone call to a whorehouse in Decatur, Illinois to see if his friend had room for one more whore.

"Hey Jimmy! I've got a bad, bad bitch here with me. She's a square and married but everything else is splendid. Do you have space for another one. She's tough though man, no shit," he grinned.

"Roger, man, you are something else. Lucky enough to shit in a swinging jug. Yeah, send her on down," he replied.

Once Peggy arrived in Decatur, she met other girls and began making friends. Before long, Peggy had started thinking the way the other whores were thinking. She made good money there.

The first month she gave Roger $2,200. She seemed to have forgotten about her husband, although she would call her mother who had her child, check on the baby and occasionally she'd send money back.

She had been introduced to the fast track; a brand new life in another world and was getting used to it. She even gave Roger much more money than he had asked for because she did not want to go back to her husband after a life she was indeed enjoying.

One day Roger took her aside and made an attempt to destroy the pictures but she objected.

"Burn this one, this one, don't burn this one, here burn this one." She was picking out the ones to keep and the ones to destroy. She kept the ones of he and she making love. This was truly Roger's action now.

Peggy turned out to be a notorious whore. She was making more money than any of the other girls in the place. She remained at that particular house for four years, with other whores coming and going.

Roger held on tight to his good thing. Besides, Peggy had fallen in love with the whoring but she didn't realize how much that pussy was worth if it was handled in the proper perspective.

Things were moving along just swell for Peggy and Roger until that fatal day when Peggy allowed somebody to stick a needle in her arm. Roger didn't play that stuff, knowing what a junkie whore was about, he came really close to hurting her.

Roger did the next best thing he could think of. He packed her up and sent her off to another whorehouse, never to see her again.

CHAPTER 12
TRUE STORIES OF PIMPS

Following, are true stories of various types of pimps and the smoothness of their operations.

1. THE KING PIMP

If the king pimp's critics could have the opportunity to see how the king pimp's operation was set up, there is no doubt they would be utterly surprised. It would strike them in the same respect that Ripley's Believe It Or Not strikes them.

The king pimp serves a much-needed purpose. It is a home for wayward whores and prostitutes - only seven or eight at a time. They all have the convenience they are normally afforded at home and more.

Usually he owns his own house with enough lovely rooms to accommodate them. You will never find a whore or a prostitute homeless or asking for help from *"Hands Across America"* unless she is an addict. King pimps don't deal with addicts.

When he does not own a house of his own, he will rent a large enough apartment to accommodate his fold. He sleeps alone in the master bedroom, usually his basement is the lolling or recreation room, complete with wall-to-wall carpet, waterbeds, wet bar, and all the fine trimmings.

Each girl will have her night with him. Each girl will bring her money to him. Each girl must understand the rules and regulations that are stipulated in their verbal contract.

Each girl has her own room and when the king pimp gets in a sexual mood, she will be notified in advance. Each *MUST* understand that she has six or seven *"wives-in-law"* and that it is just one big happy family!

There is no need to fight or have a too-heated argument. All she has to do is pay her dues. The girls can leave whenever they are dissatisfied or one might have a good night and decides to branch out on her own—that is her prerogative. That is why you might hear a king pimp say *"The story of my life, is a woman coming and a woman going."* Girls are standing in line to take the last one's place. The vacancies do not stay open long because they are treated fairly and are doing what they want to do.

The king pimp handles her jail problems, cares for her when she is ill and sees to it that she dresses in the latest fashions. She is protected from stones, slurs, and the society that doesn't understand her or her lifestyle.

If the homeless are left in the streets, a shelter is provided; if battered wives are left out, society provides shelters for battered women; but if the whore or prostitute is homeless, where can she go and feel welcome and comfortable? Squares don't want her, so who else does she have to run to. The king pimp's door is usually open and in special cases, he will make allowances.

I have no sympathy for a female unless she is elderly, sick, disabled, or pregnant. There is no need for poverty for a healthy, able-bodied young female. She doesn't have to pick up the crust that her upper-class peers toss to her. **I say and firmly believe that the first law of nature is self preservation**, as long as you are not hurting anyone. The king pimp's greatest desire is to have seven women; each one is an artist in her particular field. The booster can supply clothes for the entire fold, including and above all others, the king pimp. The pickpocket can pay the house note.

The paper hanger can pay taxes and utilities, the drag girl can take care of his cars and the three prostitutes can provide him with spending money.

The **king pimp's** duties are to rest, dress, read the funnies, collect the monies and seldom gets the honey. As I said before, instead of criticizing a king pimp, *name a man that can control seven or eight female minds at the same time, when the average layman cannot control one*. There are two ex-king pimps that still exist in Chicago. I truly wish that it was possible to take the critics of the king pimp on a tour of his domain where it could be personally witnessed as to the term *"the sleazy side of life."* But due to certain circumstances, I'll have to let the closed eyes remain closed.

2. THE UPPERCLASS PIMP

Clifford Cherry, was a man of distinction. An entrepreneur, sportsman, and a man about town, who won many awards at golf, received trophies for being one of the 10 best dressed of the Dress Horseman's Club; and outstanding man of the year.

His golf cronies were lawyers, doctors, politicians and other influential people. He played an excellent game of golf. His female companions consisted of first-class ladies of the evening and a few classy daughters of the night. The only time they were seen with him was at some major event; never in bars, street corners or second rate hotels or brothels.

His hobbies were golf or other forms of sports, shopping at his favorite haberdashery, or as a conge-

nial host at a popular Chicago night club. He owned
several automobiles including a Pierce-Arrow, he also
owned a rambling ranch-style home, lavishly furnished
in an exclusive suburb of Chicago and a summer home
in Covert, Michigan.

His supper club was where you could meet the
elites. Celebrities, tourists, and people from various
backgrounds, all stopped there to enjoy the ambiance
over dinner and cocktails. He employed thirty people,
including one of the world's greatest heavyweight boxing champ's wife, as a waitress before she married the
champ. He employed the best White and Black chefs.
He was the first Black to introduce wall-to-wall carpet-
ing in a restaurant on the south-side of Chicago.

Clifford Cherry was a boxing enthusiast and had
a keen interest in boxing. His favorite middleweight
champion had retired and made an attempt at a come-
back, but found that most of the promoters were turning thumbs down to him. He found that among his many
fair-weathered friends, he had no backers. The news
reached Clifford Cherry who had great confidence that
the retired champ could in fact regain the middleweight
championship for the fifth time. Clifford put up the
money and his entrepreneur abilities made him an instant promoter and manager.

The fighter took a few tuneups, losing one to
Ralph "Tiger" Jones but was soon facing the middleweight champion for the title. He won the fight in the
second round by a knockout, making him the new
middleweight champion, and Clifford Cherry a man to
reckon with.

There was and still are many upper-class pimps
but Clifford Cherry stood out alone. He was Chicago's
representative whenever he visited other cities. Clifford
Cherry died in the 1970's; his mourners in the thousands, consisted of both Black and White people from
all levels, backgrounds and cultures, and you could easily detect that the man was well thought of.

**NOT ALL PIMPS ARE OBNOXIOUS,
VULGAR, AND TASTELESS.**

**STACY'S MAIN MAN: WOODROW
WITH ONE OF HIS TOP WHORES'**

THE PIMP, HIS WOMEN AND THE NITE-LIFE

STACY TRADED HIS CONVERTIBLE 1961 ELDORADO
FOR THIS, HIS FIRST ROLLS ROYCE!

3. GENTLEMAN PIMP

Helen Boyd was like the wild, beautiful flowers that grow in the wilderness but was lucky enough to be plucked, vased and survive. She was one of the prettiest young women that God ever put on earth and was as ingenuous as she was stacked. She came from the wrong side of the tracks...and was a mixture of Black, Irish and Cherokee Indian. Her mother was also a very lovely woman but a shade darker in complexion and an alcoholic.

Helen Boyd came from a very poor background; 31st Street and Giles in Chicago's ghetto. When one looked at her, one could hardly believe it. She had an older sister, but her sister, Angela, was more like her mother. Helen could pass for Hispanic or Native American.

When she was in her third year in high school, at 17 years of age, she met Alonzo Collins, her first love. They started going steady and after several months, Helen became pregnant.

Helen and Alonzo told themselves that they were in love and decided to elope. Alonzo's family was very well known among the elites and couldn't afford any scandals. When Alonzo brought his new bride home to meet his family, Helen got a very cold response. Soon, the mother was researching Helen's background. She found out that Helen was from the other side of the tracks, her mother an alcoholic and a prostitute. Helen didn't even know her father, the marriage was quickly annulled with the understanding that Helen would receive child support.

Helen's pride would not let her accept the handout of child support. She made a silent vow to herself that she would show those Collins' that she could survive without their handouts. She didn't know how but she would find a way.

Her grandmother, who was seventy-five percent Cherokee, took care of Helen with her meager monthly welfare check. Her mother stayed so drunk she didn't know whether she was coming or going.

Helen's mother became very sick and Helen had to quit school and have the baby. With a sick mother, a young baby, and no job, Helen didn't know what to do. She saw Alonzo every so often, but refused to accept the offers he made in order to help his little son. She tried to work and earn a living but it was too meager to support her, her baby, her mother and her lazy sister.

So Helen did something that she never ever thought she would do. She took to the streets to earn it. With the beauty that she possessed, it didn't take her long to straighten things out on the home front.

When Helen was 18 ½ years old, her mother fell out of a window and broke her neck. Some speculated it was suicide, some suspected she was drunk and fell.

Helen really turned out when she became an outlaw whore. The money was coming in good but the news got around about how much money she was making and didn't have a pimp. In those days, outlaw whores didn't have a chance. The renegade, hypocrite, transporting and blackmailing pimps ears were open and it was open season on Helen. When she refused their offers, they would manhandle her, put their broads on her and take her money.

One night, three tough street girls beat her, scratched her pretty face up and took $500 from her. She tried to change neighborhoods for other strolls but the same thing happened.

She was so disgusted she almost chose one of the worst type of pimps. But faith saved her, she got sick and it was discovered that she had Tuberculosis. She was sent to the TB Sanitarium on North Pulaski Street in Chicago.

While there, she met Rodney who was a pimp

of consequence. They became intimate, soon got together, swapped experiences and became very fond of each other.

He would always remind her that a man without a woman is like a woman without a man, they are both lost. Her TB case cleared up and she was released. But Rodney stayed with her, she was faithful to him; visiting him often, taking him money and gifts, letting him know how much she needed and cared about him; and she was proving it.

Rodney was released from the sanitarium, and he and Helen rented a big apartment. He found her a brothel to work in that paid good money and worked mostly white girls. No house madam would have turned Helen down. Now that she had protection and connections, it seemed like brothels lit up when the customers found out about the little Indian squaw.

Her take was always $1,000 every two weeks or better. Rodney was a gentleman. He always brought her gifts and made sure her son was well taken care of and attended school while she was away.

They saved together, brought a new Cadillac and replenished her wardrobe. In the next eight years, they were able to put $20,000 down on an eight-flat building.

Rodney only had to slap her back to reality once in the entire eight years; the next eight years, her son had completed college, left home, got married, and ran for public office. They lived as man and wife for the next four years until Rodney died.

Helen's loss of Rodney took quite a toll on her and hurt more than it did when her mother died.

BEHIND EVERY GOOD MAN IS A GOOD WOMAN. SO YOU SEE, THERE IS A GOOD SIDE TO PIMPING.

4. MACK-MAN

During the 1700's, pretty women and young beautiful girls were coming from all directions looking for work as saloon girls. The shrewd businessmen organized a twelve man committee that raised the question on how to capitalize from the rare combination of women and alcohol? It did not take long before there were more saloons built providing more employment for saloon girls.

The girls worked for the establishment only; there was no other connection between the saloon girls and the mack-men. An exchange of the girls from one saloon to another would be made when the clientele became a bit too tired of the same girls.

They went from saloon to saloon, seeking employment. Then came the cathouses (brothels), then it was from brothel to brothel. Now it's from coast to coast, all over the nation, the mack-men just took over big-time prostitution.

"Hey Bill, how are things in the sun?" asked Charlie of Cleveland.

"What the hell, I was just thinking about coming out there next week," said Bill from Los Angeles.

"How's tricks going in that town? I called Kansas City and Chicago last week, the rest of the boys seem to be raking it in real good," said Charlie.

"Well you know there is always enough here Charlie, this is close to Tinsel Town. Are you situated with fresh girls?" Bill asked.

"Oh what the hell, I could stand a couple of blondes and one very pretty black one," Charlie told him.

"Okay Charlie, look for it next week and in the meantime, call Arizona and a few other places, except

New York. I just checked that out. See how things are," Bill explained.

Back in Los Angeles, Allie told Rose to send two blondes and a pretty black girl to Charlie Ross in Cleveland.

"Tell them to stay for a month," Bill told his stooge.

In two weeks the girls were there. That's how the mack-men operate. One of the thorns in the side of mack-men was the "mack-maniacs."

Sometimes a young girl is stopped, picked up and not seen again for a very long time, if ever. She is being flown from one part of the country to the other. The mack-maniac isn't such a nice guy.

5. GIGOLO

Kevin, even as an adolescent on into adulthood, was always considered a very tall, handsome, blond, blue-eyed young man. He had charisma and was exotic and witty. He was always a lot of fun but was shy when it came to dealing with females.

As a young man, he worked as a stock boy at the local grocery store. The neighborhood girls and young women would usually tease him because they knew of his shyness.

One day, he was told to carry an order to a customer because of her illness. When he got to the house, he was greeted by an obviously wealthy, rather older lady. The lady had a guest, another older lady.

"Come right in young man," said the well-kept and polished matron."

Kevin was 6'3" tall, his shirt sleeves were rolled up and the basket was on his shoulder. He took the groceries to the kitchen and placed them where she asked. The other guest couldn't take her eyes off Kevin.

She followed him with her eyes as he moved

around the kitchen. Finally, she got up and walked into
the kitchen with a gold and pearl cigarette holder dan-
gling between her fingers. One could easily guess she
was from the right side of the tracks.

"Hi!" she hissed to Kevin.

"Hi!" Kevin countered.

The lady of the house gave Kevin a generous
tip, he thanked her and left.

After Kevin had left, the two ladies sat down to
finish their tea.

"Does he live in this neighborhood?" the guest
asked.

"I don't know him," said the lady of the house.

"Well, I really wouldn't mind having him for an
escort. He is really something to look at. He reminds
me of Bob when he was younger," the old hen said as
they chuckled together.

After about a month, the guest contacted her
hostess and inquired about that little male doll, Kevin.

"As a matter of fact, Ethel, when you called I
was thinking about you. Yes, I saw your little male doll
yesterday. He brought over some groceries for me,"
they chuckled.

"Katie, the annual dinner dance for the Country Club is this Friday night and I do need an escort. It
would be just divine to have that gorgeous hunk of a
man as my escort to make the other gals a little jealous.
Do you think he would mind being seen with an old bat
like me?"

"I'd make arrangements for a complete outfit
for him to wear and of course I'd make it worth his
while monetarily. Do you think he would go for it?"

"Well you talk to him for me and give me a call
back. I'll be waiting patiently by the phone."

When Katie called the grocery order in, Kevin
raced to prepare the order because the lady gave great
tips. Upon arriving with her order, Kevin was greeted

warmly at the door and Katie smiled and asked, "How's my boy today?"

"Fine ma'am, just fine," Kevin replied.

Katie didn't like small talk and got right to the subject. "Kevin, do you remember the day you delivered groceries, over a month ago, and a lady friend of mine was visiting and she asked you your name?" Katie asked.

Kevin replied, "Oh yes ma'am I remember her."

Katie continued in a controlled and warm voice, "Well, Ethel, that's her name, is attending a big social event this Friday night and she is afraid of going alone with all the mugging and so forth going on. She is willing to purchase your attire for the evening in addition to giving you a generous tip for your time if you escort her."

Kevin, rather taken aback, replied in an excited voice, "You mean she wants me to escort her to the social shindig? She's such a nice lady, of course, I'd escort her but she wouldn't have to pay me, I'd be happy to go."

"Well, telephone me here tomorrow around 3:00 p.m. and I'll have a message for you," Katie told Kevin.

The next day, promptly at 3 o'clock, Kevin telephoned Katie. Katie asked Kevin, "When you get off work, would you please stop by my house so we can have a talk?"

"Sure thing," Kevin replied.

When Kevin arrived, Katie briefed him on the evening and then she gave him a sealed envelope saying, "She told me to tell you to go out and buy yourself a complete outfit for the evening, from the shoes to the overcoat or whatever you need and she will see you on Friday at her home. Here's her address and telephone number."

Kevin took the envelope and thanked Katie. When he was in the confines of his car, Kevin opened the envelope. To his surprise and utter amazement, there were ten $100 bills staring out at him.

"Oh my God, oh my God." Kevin could not believe his new found fortune.

The next day, Kevin rushed downtown and purchased all the right clothes for his Friday social whirl with Mrs. Ethel Pearson.

Upon returning from his shopping spree, Kevin telephoned Mrs. Pearson to inform her how he had spent the money.

Her reply was,"Did I give you enough money? And don't call me Mrs. Pearson in public, call me Ethel, okay?"

Kevin stammered "Yes ma'am, Mrs. Pearson, yes you did, and I want to thank you for everything, uh I mean Ethel and I won't forget to call you Ethel."

Ethel smiled and said "Kevin, catch a cab to this address at exactly 6:00 p.m. tomorrow. Can you drive?"

"Yes ma'am, I can drive very well and I'll be there on time," he told her.

That Friday, Mrs. Pearson was standing in the window when Kevin pulled up in a Yellow cab. Kevin paid the driver, got out and she greeted him at the door.

Ethel scrutinized Kevin's new look in one sweeping glance of her practiced eyes and very much liked what she saw. Kevin had style, class and good taste and looked as though he had just stepped out of Hollywood. She would definitely feel proud being in the company of such a handsome young man.

Mrs. Pearson was a widower. Her deceased husband, Robert A. Pearson, had been the president of Pearson Paint Co., Inc. and had left his entire estate to her, his wife. She had no financial problems.

Ethel gave Kevin a tour of her palatial home with statues, water fountains, expensive oils on canvas of her and her late husband, whose resemblance as a young man was striking to Kevin's.

Ethel could not resist saying, "Kevin, now you can see why I chose you to be my escort tonight."

Kevin smiled as he spoke, "He even combed his hair in my style."

Before they departed the mansion, Ethel put Kevin through a *"secret manners test."*

"Well, young man, are you ready? Here are the keys to the car." Immediately Kevin started towards the door.

Like all young men when it comes to driving expensive cars, Kevin was no exception at 19 ½ years old. Mrs. Pearson was on her own. No car door opened for her. Later she would tutor him in areas he was lax.

On the way to the affair, they discussed several topics, including Kevin's education; he was thinking of becoming an attorney.

Just before reaching their destination, Ethel Pearson thought perhaps she should give Kevin a pep talk.

She started, "Kevin dear, you are about to enter a new field. Where we're going tonight, you will meet sophisticated, rich, prominent and important women. For sure some of those same rich women will slip you their telephone number or a card. Take the number and be cordial; you will be well rewarded. Do you realize you could make a career of what you are doing now and maybe modeling too? You would have an enviable income."

Kevin replied looking quite puzzled, "I don't understand Mrs. Pearson."

"You see that's your first mistake! I explained to you before we left home not to ever call me Mrs. Pearson.

It's Ethel, honey, Ethel. And while we're at it, I may as well acquaint you with some other little tidbits of how to gain points with ladies. Never come to pickup a lady without bringing her candy, flowers or a warm card; she wants to show off to her friends what a thoughtful young man her escort is. When you are with these old hens, it will be something like restoration of youth to them to be seen with such a handsome, witty and well-dressed young man."

Kevin grinned because he had never heard talk like this before.

"Kevin, dear, you must learn manners - how to dress, how to display your gentlemanship towards the lady that you are escorting; that in itself will be your calling card. You will be paid generously and maybe a little later you might want to open an escort service."

A couple of the old girls were standing outside when he pulled the Bentley to a stop; got out, went around and assisted Ethel out of the car. Their eyes widened as they dashed inside to spread the news of Ethel Pearson's handsome escort.

The first time Kevin felt nervous was when they walked in, everybody was talking and all of a sudden all conversation hushed and all eyes fell on Kevin and Ethel Pearson. It didn't take long for the crowd to discover they were staring as Kevin took Ethel's coat. Conversation resumed and Kevin and Ethel found they had lots of company seated around them.

Ethel, of course was quite pleased to introduce Kevin Sprott to Vera, Doris, Susie and Paula to name a few of the gaping women. Kevin made quite a hit that night, dancing with all the ladies, snapping pictures, exchanging tales, lots of laughter and Dom Perigon flowing everywhere.

Kevin didn't have to say a word. The women were doing it all for him. Three at one time giving him their telephone numbers and pleading for him to call

them, and soon, telling him that it would be worth his
while. Kevin caught on fast, as the thought of getting
rich while having a good time was dancing in his head.

On the way back to Ethel's house she chatted
about how much the *"girls"* admired him. She also gave
him another $1,000 after he saw her safely home and
told him not to forget to call her. His father and mother
quizzed him about the clothes but he lied with a cover-
up story about a part-time job of driving an old lady
around that paid more money than the store. They
believed him. The next thing he had to do was quit his
job and try his hand at the escort service.

Kevin walked into the store two hours late the
following morning and went straight to the stockroom.

"Hey Mike, what did old man Cooper say when
I didn't show up on time this morning?" Kevin asked.

Mike had taken his gloves off and was standing
there flabbergasted.

"Kevin, he said, "where did you get the new
duds? What's happening? Oh, Mr. Cooper said he had
a surprise for you."

"I have a surprise for him too," Kevin added as
he reached in his pocket and started counting fifty dollar bills.

"I'm quitting, I'm going into business for myself
and you can be my partner Mike, if you'd like."

Mike, who by now was goggle-eyed after seeing
all those fifty dollar bills asked excitedly, "What kind of
business are we going into?"

Kevin told him, "An escort service. All we have
to do is drive little, old, rich ladies around, they pay
good and most of them are widows."

That's pimping. You are a pimping bastard. They
call your kind of pimping a gi..gi..gig..gig..gigolo." Mike
finally stuttered out.

"No, no, no" Kevin screamed. "There's a difference between what you are talking about and an escort

service."

"Well that's not the way I hear it. Anybody that accepts money from a female, he's in some form of pimping. No, Kevin, I don't care to be a pimp," Mike told Kevin.

"Okay Mike, you just stay here and count the Campbell Soup cans and I'll see you around." Kevin left to go to the office and tell old man Cooper that he had found himself a better job.

Cooper tried to dissuade Kevin by telling him he should stay on and get promoted to the front office but Kevin said "Thanks but no thanks. I've got to try this out to see if it works for me."

"Okay, gigolo," Cooper said, "you have my blessing."

Kevin smiled and he left and didn't look back. Move forward, he certainly did. His escort service/model agency took off overnight and became the biggest in the Chicago area.

Chapter 13
ARTICLES FOUND IN REGIONAL NEWSPAPERS

CITY SEEKS BREAKS FOR PIMPS AND PROSTITUTES:
by Edward G. Morris, Atlantic City, New Jersey.

The city's top law enforcement officials say that they would like to let prostitutes work in their homes, undisturbed, if they agree to conduct their business indoors, do not disturb their neighbors and register with the police.

"We are trying to find some way to control prostitution, using minimum manpower and reduced costs to the city," said Police Commissioner John Rodrick and Public Safety Commissioner Willie Clayton, both in favor of decriminalizing prostitution.

"Enforcing laws against prostitution have never worked and will never work," Clayton said.

"Men and women were born with three biological drives- hunger, thirst, and sex. We have not been successful in trying to legislate hunger or thirst, and we are not doing a good job with sex."

Prostitution has always been a problem in Atlantic City, however, it has grown with the influx of casinos.

Residents and tourists complain that prostitutes unabashedly block cars on Pacific Avenue and even jump in cars that stop at traffic lights.

The officials proposed that prostitutes who agree to be fingerprinted and photographed would be permitted to operate out of their own homes, 'If the neighbors do not complain.' If spotted on the street or in casinos they would be identified by the their registration number and arrested.

"We should not have to tie up our manpower and our money, chasing them up and down Pacific Avenue," the Commissioner said.

ATLANTA IS ON RIGHT TRACK IN HANDLING PROSTITUTION:
by James J Kilpatrick

Like many other cities around the nation, Atlanta has had a vexatious problem with prostitution. Mayor Andrew Young appointed a committee to make recommendations to deal with it. The committee delivered a remarkably sensible report on a sensible subject.

The key recommendation stated, more implicitly than explicitly: "Prostitutes in Atlanta should be allowed to work out of escort services, bars and hotels, as long as they do so discreetly and stay off the streets. Prostitution should be effectively decriminalized. If prostitutes agree to be tested regularly for sexually transmitted diseases, including AIDS, penalties would be reduced or eliminated."

The recommendations were initially drafted by Peter Whiteside, a business consultant. He explained his reasoning to the Atlanta Journal and Constitution in the following words,"It is a matter of management, if you operate out of well run escort services, or you operate out of a bar or from a beeper, and you stay out of public areas where you are not wanted, then the general society would not mind. A lot of high class call girls operate out of hotels and nobody ever notices that they are call girls. They don't hurt anybody."

Whiteside made one more point: "Atlanta gets no tax revenues from unregulated prostitution, but the licensed escort services pay local taxes and keep the kind of records from which income taxes could be derived. It is a thought."

Mayor Young's 14-member task force considered recommendations from one extreme to the other. Some witnesses called for an all-out crackdown on prostitution accompanied by harsher laws and stiffer penalties. One proposal was to get tough with the prostitutes' customers and to publicize their names when arrested. At the other extreme were proposals to totally legalize prostitution but to confine it to the red-light districts.

The Mayor's committee came down in a sensible, ambivalent, middle position. Prostitution will continue to go *"against the law"* but the law would be enforced only against women (and against male prostitutes as well) who publicly make a nuisance of themselves. This recommendation attacked the community problem and left the moral issues for another day.

The English poet, Bertrand Russell, once remarked that; "Prostitution, as it exists in Christian countries, is an exceedingly undesirable career."

Thousands of women manifestly do not agree with him. The Mayflower Madam in New York had no trouble recruiting women of beauty and some degree of intelligence.

There isn't a city in the nation, or many small towns, without some women for hire. In Washington, the police wearily maintain a running battle with the 14th Street girls but they recognize that their aim is only to contain the traffic, they have no hope of stamping it out completely. Too many girls, not enough cops.

The law has enough to worry about without worrying over discreet sexual relations between consenting adults. Brazen public conduct can't be tolerated of course, and police can't be expected to look the other way while decent neighborhoods are destroyed. But Atlanta's Task Force has the right idea: Let the ancient law of supply and demand quietly accommodate the oldest profession in the world.

CONSIDER LEGALIZING PROSTITUTION:
CANADA WOULD ALLOW HOOKER TO OPERATE OUT OF THEIR HOMES
Ottawa, Canada (UPI)

Canada is considering legalizing prostitution and allowing hookers to operate out of their homes as part of legislation aimed at curbing street soliciting, the government said this week.

Justice Minister John Crosby, whose department will prepare new laws to be introduced this fall, to deal with both pornography and prostitution said he will consider legalizing prostitution if it was acceptable to the majority of Canadians.

"We all know this is a problem that has been with society for hundreds of years," Crosby said. "We should deal with the problem in a sensible manner."

Crosby was responding to a 750-page report by a government committee on pornography and prostitution that included a recommendation to remove prostitution activities from the Criminal Code.

The committee also recommended legal prostitution establishments, operated by one or two prostitutes, age 18 years or older, operated by municipal authorities. Crosby said surveys carried out by his department showed that most Canadians would accept legalized prostitution.

Prostitution is not a crime in Canada but the Criminal Code prohibits a number of related activities, including soliciting, procuring, living off its proceeds and keeping a house of prostitution. The government's proposed legislation dealing with street soliciting will make it clear that any kind of soliciting, even if its not pressing or persistent, is illegal. Metropolitan cities in Canada have complained for months that street soliciting was contributing to the decay of downtown areas.

Crosby also said he would not rule out so-called *"red-light districts"* where prostitutes can comfortably ply their trade. The committee which studied prostitution in several countries found that the United States has *"the most draconian provision against such activities but no effective control of the problem."*

The best short-term solution, according to the report, was found in Denmark where prostitution is operated as a regular business, and the Netherlands, where there is a mix of criminal law and specific brothel locations.

The committee also recommended expanding the definition of hate literature in the Criminal Code to include graphic representations that promote hatred of either sex, criminal sanctions against violent material that is not sexually explicit and regulation of live performances.

The committee took a feminist approach to pornography, recommending harsher penalties for violent and degrading sex and proposing that so-called *"soft pornography, publications and video tapes"* that are sexually explicit but not degrading be subject to display and access restrictions.

PIMPING IS FINE IF WOMEN ARE TREATED WELL: PANEL

There was good news recently for pimps in London, England, and pimps in the United States would benefit from news in the same way, if only the head of state could become more modernized.

A panel of probation officers, admitting its conclusion would prove *"highly controversial"* saying *"there is nothing wrong with a pimp living off the earnings of a prostitute if he treats her well."*

"It is not an offense for a girl to earn her living by prostitution and therefore I do not believe it should be an offense for a man whom she is living with to live off her earnings, unless he coerces her or uses violence or threats" said Murray Bruggen, Chairman of the National Association of Probation Officers.

Wake up America, you are dragging your feet!

INDICTED LOS ANGELES MAN IN PROBE OF HOOKERS' PIMPS

In what was announced as a major crackdown on the men who earned their living from prostitutes, a Los Angeles man was recently arrested and charged with pimping in San Francisco.

Alexander McKenzie, 26, was arrested following a grand jury indictment against him. He was the first person caught under the crackdown which District Attorney Joseph Freitas, Jr. announced several weeks ago after meeting with community groups.

On testimony from three prostitutes, ages 17, 20, and 22 said they produced $300 a day and turned it over to McKenzie and added that they had no other talent for them to earn $300 a day.

WHY PROSTITUTION SHOULD BE LEGALIZED

Speaking of legalizing prostitution, it is obvious why it is not legal. Anything that can not be taxed in America is illegal. If the system could tax drugs it would be legal. They may as well legalize prostitution because they will never be able to stop it. They, whoever they are, would come closer to making a race horse out of a donkey, than to stop a woman from making her living by selling her body; it's a means of survival for the unfortunate. Not even the deadly AIDS virus can stop it. Why not legalize it? It serves a purpose, can you imagine how many men don't have a wife or even a girlfriend. There are various reasons why prostitution should be legalized; what are these men supposed to do for sex? Sex is important to man as food is to a hungry stomach, water is to a thirsty mouth and sleep is to a tired individual. To take sex away from a man is like leaving a dog in a meat house and advising him not to eat any of the meat. By legalizing prostitution, it will prevent most rapes, killing of prostitutes, and it will save on divorces, when a man can add variety to his sex life.

The way this system is set up it is too difficult. Whiskey, cigarettes, and guns are all legal and they are the world's number one killers. What harm can prostitution cause other than serve a very important purpose. It gives man one of the greatest feelings of all times and the system wants to force man to do without it. Even Ray Charles and Stevie Wonder can see that is not going to work as an alternative to rape. But if man knows where he can go and have some nice clean fun with a prostitute, what more can man ask for. Some people must wonder why most tricks and Johns target prostitutes to kill and mutilate, there are various reasons but one is the mind of a man who doesn't have sex at his disposal. After having sex with a prostitute, the disturbed man's mind may flash back, and realize that when she is finished with him she goes to the next man and he tells himself: *"as good as she made me feel, she will never go to another man"* then kills her.

If prostitution was legalized, the prostitute could have *protection and connection* by working in a house of pleasure. The male donkey kicks the female donkey when he reaches a climax, she made him feel too good. When I was pimping, I knew that I had the whole world beat, because I was selling something that even the birds and the bees loved. Some people sold clothing, groceries, alcoholic beverages, drugs, houses, cars, etc., but they all had to come by my house, because I had something that they really wanted *THE SUGAR BOWL*.

You must understand that prostitution is like Hollywood. The leading lady is the star and they built her a stage to perform on, her fans are her audience and they must pay before they see the show. The same thing happens in the asphalt jungle where the whore is the star and the world is her stage, her tricks are her audience and they must also pay before she performs, her pimp is her manager and is the director of the show.

If President Clinton was to realize how important the whore and prostitutes were to humanity, with his youthful and new way of thinking there is no doubt in my mind that he would consider legalizing prostitution. Those old lawmakers are just too old to understand. They can't see the forest for the trees. They actually believe, that they can stop prostitution - the oldest profession in the world. How can they stop it, yet they can't stop wars? The pimp and the whore will be around long after those type of old warped-minded politicians are dead and gone. The pimp is to the whore what the husband is to the wife, the secretary to the executive, the doctor to the nurse, the president to the first lady and the king to his queen. Prostitution is legal in London and some of the states in the US, as long as the woman is not forced into it.

Wake up America, you are dragging your feet!

Chapter 14
A MESSAGE TO THE YOUTH OF AMERICA

READ! READ! READ! Reading, writing and arithmetic are still the core of any pertinent education in America. Particularly reading.

It is with sorrow that we note that a regional high school in Massachusetts is eliminating its Summer reading program for 898 advanced and honor students. Part of the reason being is because the program books are *"trash and become boring."* But I believe education is in all books.

There are many current events that students should learn. It would be important to construct textbooks for young girls explaining to them how to be aware of undesirable young men.

This chapter shows that there are many facets of life that desperately need to be elaborated on.

There is a piece of education in every book. If education means anything, the adults who run schools should take a stance against cutting the reading load of students.

To let students shy away from reading is cruel by the grown-ups who are in charge of their future. At this point, students can trigger their imagination through the written word students can discover boundless and exciting expansions of the mind, - which ALL books represent.

Also at this point, maybe through writing, their penned words may make interesting reading for others. It is accepted that there are boring and dull books, yet they still render some form of education.

"The Sweet Science of Sin" turns the record over and the title is "Our Society."

The deaths of Len Bias and Don Rogers were published and circulated all over the nation because of their popularity in sports. Naturally, that is just the tip of the iceberg, there are millions of other deaths that are attributed to cocaine abuse that this nation will never hear or read about due to their *"insignificance."* There have been reports that it is not the cocaine that kills, but the chemicals and mixtures with which it is manufactured.

It is accepted that some people are not as mentally and physically strong as others, but as the old saying goes, *"the strong survive and the weak perish."*

My advice to the youth of today is to push for strength. God and the devil are constantly at work, trying to see who can win the most souls. But God has said, *"Before the devil has more souls than Him, He will turn all souls to stones."*

Peer pressure, oppression, stress, fear of being called a square, and wanting to be hip are responsible for a lot of youths going astray. But I believe you are not hip, until you are hip to the Man upstairs. One of the major mistakes American parents make is to confront their children about drugs without knowing the facts. As my naive mother use to say: *"Don't shoot no reefer in my house."*

The youths quickly realize that when their parents, make those type of remarks, they certainly do not know what they are talking about. The youth may be led to believe that maybe his peers are right when he or she tells him that it is alright to do drugs.

Refrain from alcohol and drug abuse. Go back to school if you are a drop-out; remain if you are there. Get involved in sports, give yourself a chance - you owe it to yourself. Doing drugs, selling drugs, stealing, pimping or prostituting are going to be obsolete in the coming years.

If you don't heed what I'm saying, you will be left out in the cold. Today drug use is mostly epidemic. Today's and tomorrow's heartache for all people are hard drugs.

I would be deeply grateful if this book would be instrumental in enlightening the American people and the youth of today, - tomorrow's people.

I sincerely wish that this book would serve as both a personal and a general history guide; an overview of living in the ghettos.

I've never felt as great as I feel now; now that I have been blessed to witness my golden anniversary and most of my life is behind me.

The versatility that life itself offers is challenging. I enjoy being able to sit here and write and warn our future leaders. It gives me great pride to be able to consider myself a contributing factor for some facets of mankind.

As I speak through my mind and fingers to the youth of the present and future; learn to be versatile; while traveling down the road of life, so you won't get boxed in a corner.

Speaking to our young of America, in case you are climbing a high and steep mountain, never look down, for you might get nervous and fall. While leading in the race of life, never look back because someone might be gaining on you.

Three-fourths of the miseries and misunderstanding in the world will disappear if we step into the shoes of our advisors and understand their viewpoint. We will then agree with them or think of them charitably. Good laws lead to the making of better ones and bad laws bring about worse.

The one time when you are not critical of either the voice or the tunes is when someone is singing you

THE LATE GREAT DUKE ELLINGTON -
RUBBING SHOULDERS WITH PIMPS AND PROSTITUTES

praises. The youngster who disobeys his parents is sure to have disobedient offspring. You are confused, but don't feel alone. Welcome to the club, there are multitudes.

To say I'm surprised at today's generation would be telling a lie, because the Holy Bible warns that the world would become more wicked and wise. That day is nearer than one might think.

In everyone's life there comes a time when we all will cry out for guidance, discipline and advice, but when you become too big-headed that you flatly refuse to accept these three essentials of life, then you are headed down the road of no return.

All men and women of influential life status have advisors. Just hope and pray that the advisors of your choice are on the positive side. The fact being that the youths of the present and future will have someone to pattern their lives after.

The majority of humanity has had an idol at one time or another - a father, a big brother image, someone to look up to. But the child whose roots are in the ghetto does not have much of a choice, the most he or she sees are thieves, stick-up men, dope-pushers, cutthroats, prostitutes, bandits and pimps; only the infamous, the ones who ride around in their fine new BMWs, Lincolns, Mercedes and Cadillacs, dripping in diamonds, gold chains and other finery who never worked a day in their lives for any of that.

Black leaders, entertainers, politicians, and sports figures do not have a sincere desire to rub shoulders with a ghetto kid. They may come around ever so often, pick up a ghetto child for publicity purposes, but are relieved when the chore is over.

The only people that the ghetto kids see that are black and have a smidgen of power is the black policeman chasing them. So it's a hard fight for the poor boy

or girl who lives in the ghetto, whether he or she is
Black, White or Hispanic.

Don't allow yourself to be caught up in the devil's
trickery - I've been there and back. I was just blessed
to be able to be here to relate my story to you.

If I had the opportunity to do it all over again, I
would train my brain in a more constructive direction.
I have often heard a famous preacher say, *"Don't do as
I do, but do as I say."* He was a messenger then, I am a
messenger now.

To my audience - please don't try to follow my
path because it's a vile path to follow. You are young
and you must be strong in heart, spirit, and mind. You,
yourself are the most beautiful person in the world. To
quote another famous preacher, *"You are somebody, for
you are a SHINING STAR and that is what you follow."*

It is gracefully accepted that sometimes it's very
difficult to find a job and have some of the nice things in
life but your darkest hour is just before dawn. Under
every dark cloud there is always a silver lining.

Just when you have lost faith and everything
seems doomed and you are about to quit, that is the
time when you are just beginning to win, because the
last hurdle that you must jump over always seems the
highest.

It has been said that if you have brains and am-
bition, money and other good things will come on their
own. Money is the freest thing in the world.

Someone has always given you money, whether
you work for it, beg for it, steal and sell for it, stick up
for it, pimp or prostitute for it. Whatever road you se-
lect in life, someone has to give you money because
I'm sure you don't have a money-making machine.

Believe me, the best things in life are free - eating and sleeping. Sure, a rat or roach eats and sleeps;
but, you want more out of life than just eating and sleeping. And <u>you</u> who are sinning; the scriptures say *"Thou*

shall not WANT." He will supply all your needs.

1.   Water - cleanliness is next to Godliness. Water cleans you externally and internally. Cools you off while quenching your thirst. You can exercise in it (swim and frolic) you can make medicine from it, beverages from it, you can search for food in it -isn't it most wonderful?

2.   Food - it's grown from the ground, sent to you by your Divine Master. This is one of the reasons so many people are becoming vegetarians. Our ancestors worked very hard to see that you eat. We are told not to eat the carcass. Our chickens, fish and cattle are essential for the meat eaters (for sins are forgiven).

3.   Clothing - we can make our own. Clothes only make a person in appearance, what's inside is what's important.

4.   Shelter - the meadows can serve as a bed in the summer months, a cave in the winter months, the daylight will serve as your electricity and the dark is for slumber -in order to survive.

5.   Women - we all must realize that God created a mate for each of his creations, and if He made anything that could give the male specimen more pleasure, then He certainly kept it in heaven.

So, you see, the best things in life are <u>free.</u>

The eyes are the windows to the heart. You can spot the good and evil by looking in the windows. It's a shame that we flatly refuse to buckle down and unite with love. We should try and understand each other's shortcomings and be able to stand together because divided we are sure to fall. I was so happy when part of the world reached out and loaned a shoulder to the starving women, men and children in the recent "We are the World" and "Hands Across America" projects.

Some people have everybody and everything - doctors, lawyers, policemen, firemen, gays, blacks, whites, prostitutes and pimps. But we are all God's children, hate is a cancer. Never allow yourself to hate; never have a vacancy for it. And if you are the young man or young woman who I think you are and want to be, then you will fight your way out of your unpleasant situation. It has been done many, many times before, only fools remain the same.

A fool is a person with both feet firmly planted in the air. We all have heard of the *"three wise men,"* but can you distinguish the difference between the wise man and the fool. There is as much difference between a wise man and a fool as there is high-noon and midnight. *"It would be better to have a thousand wise men for enemies than to have one fool for a friend"*- (King Solomon).

A wise man will change, but a fool will never change because he has only one road to travel down and that is the road of no return -hell. If you whisper wisdom in the ear of a fool, he or she will soon despise you. Jesus came on earth to heal the sick, make the lame walk, and the blind see, teach the wise wisdom, but left the fool as he found him. He who has graduated from the cycles of life, is considered wise because as a rule, youth is wasted on the young. If you had the wisdom of your parents and fore-parents, it would be too heavy a burden and the scriptures say that God will not give you a burden that you cannot bear.

Learning, know-how, and education can be acquired by experiencing and existing alone, but to acquire *WISDOM* you must greet your Golden Anniversary and that will come when you reach the age of 50 years. The problem is, we all think we are wise, the drunk thinks you are a drunk, the insane thinks you are insane, but you must pay your dues by enduring the cycles of life.

You once loved toys such as electric trains, marbles, skates, dolls and bikes, but later it became something entirely different. If God blesses you to live to be 50 years old, your life will come anew. There are different cycles in life that we must experience for the first time. If you are blessed to become 50 years old, you have, truly been blessed and are considered *WISE*.

Allowances can be made for young fools. Being at the fool's age of youth is a disastrous period of life, but to grow to become an old fool is a tragedy.

How many of your loved ones or friends have fallen by the wayside and never had the opportunity to enjoy the golden years that God prepared for his chosen few?

Never mock or make laughter at your elders because they have become gray. For she or he has been blessed. Every gray hair represents a streak of wisdom.

We don't always get out of life what we ask for, but we do pray for it. Your prayers are definitely heard and answered, but only in disguise of a dream, vision, or an idea. Because if God would come down on earth and present you with your wish, your heart wouldn't be strong enough to accept it.

How many times have you thought or dreamed of an idea and refused to follow through, and someone else took the same idea and got over? Believe in yourself. You could have done something, but you let the devil intervene. Sometimes mental and physical laziness gets in the way. Don't allow the *"Doubting Thomas'"* to discourage you by saying, *"Ah, you can't do that or you can't do this,"* consider that a challenge, and prove them wrong.

The devil and a fool are very good friends and are constantly at work. Never underestimate your fellow man, always overestimate them, because even water will seek its own level. Give them enough rope and they will hang themselves. That's the way God trapped the devil. The road to hell was paved with good intentions. The devil underestimated God, he (the devil) was caught sprinkling brimstone on the road to hell, so God gave him a permanent position -the king of hell. The devil is a miserable soul and misery loves company, so he is constantly beckoning for you.

Wisdom, wisdom, wisdom, oh how it is needed, appreciated and admired by many. Contentment and peace are the greatest riches, trust is a great gift of quality, but the greatest of all gifts is the love of GOD. None of us are wise (hip) until he is wise (hip) to the one upstairs.

Like I said before, I have all the answers, because I have been asked all the questions. Most of the subjects that I speak on aren't heard in high schools, colleges, universities and a very few churches. They only teach the guideline of the American system, but America is just one country and this is a wide, wide, world.

You see, God gave us two ears to make sure you listen and one mouth to keep shut, for when you talk you teach, when you listen you learn. Now it doesn't make you dumb when you learn something that you didn't know, it makes you smarter today than you were yesterday. Did you know that the old fable that a man had one less rib than a woman, is a lie. We all have the same. Or did you know, that the red cape that the matador uses when fighting the bull, is to attract the audience, because bulls are color blind? Or did you know that silver nitrate is put in every new born babies eyes because it is believed that every mother has or may have had gonorrhea, silver nitrate doesn't serve any purpose. Or did you know there are 1,440 minutes in a day, 168 hours in a week? Or did you know, that the milk that we and our babies drink, is not for humans, but for calves, so you see you are already a bit smarter TODAY than you were YESTERDAY.

ONE TO REMEMBER !!

They crowned him the king of pimps in 1968
Some people think he still can do it
But he thinks it's a little too late
Because at forty-nine,
It's about time for him to rest his crown
It hurt him and it saddened him when they
laid Woodrow in the ground!
But at thirty-five, it was no jive
He could stop and cop at will
But in life, if "mother nature don't get you
Then father time will!

He was the only pimp that you'll ever know
Who had a hundred broads or more
His real name is Alfred Gholson
But his peers call him Bilbo!
He rode the crest of a pimp's success
And had plenty of glitter and shine
Hollywood should have made a movie of him in his
prime.

A true pimp is something that the world may never
know
*Because only three would understand -**God,***
another pimp and a whore!
A pimp is a distinctive character, with an
exceptional intellect Who possesses the ability to
deal with the most difficult task
With the greatest of ease,
And all of his lady friends are very much pleased!

A pimp's career is like all other careers,
There is always an end
But true pimps don't ever give up
Because there is another career awaiting just around
the bend!

Now some people have been curious to know about
that rich white lady that came over looking for super
black sex,
When Bilbo read a page to her out of his text,
"Now Miss Ann, you'll have to play by the rules,
Because I an not one of those god-damn fools
You are going to have to pay me and pay me at will,
because you are not one third as pretty as a thousand
dollar bill!

Bilbo always went by his mentor's sayings,
The one that does the choosing does the paying,
The story of his life has been
A woman coming and a woman going,
Because staying with one over four years
Becomes sort of boring!

The separation between him and the white lady,
A lot were glad she left, but what they didn't know is
They wasn't one third as glad as he was himself!
Bet wherever she is and whoever she's with,
I'm sure Bilbo is in the will, because the love and sex
knot that Bilbo tied, is tied tight and very, very, still!

Because he taught her something
That schools, colleges and universities forget to
teach,
How to play with fools
But Bilbo's kind don't ever reach
he taught them to have no mercy on fools
They are like chicken and sheep,
All they want is to sleep and fuck
And that's why God put them on earth for women to
shear and pluck!
Now Bilbo's castle has crumbled,
He refuses to look back,
And see that the
type of ladies he deals with today are a little slow for
such a track!

By: Mr. Alfred "Bilbo" Gholson

The **SWEET SCIENCE OF SIN** is here to educate America. Mr. Alfred "Bilbo" Gholson, said *"he must have set a blazing trail in the world of pimps and prostitutes being involved with twenty-three females at one time."*

Now he has reached the age and stage where his past lifestyle has become un-becoming to him, but he breaks his silence since every other infamous facet has opened their closet doors.

The true sides of the world of pimps and prostitutes have never been told. People have been awarded Ph.D.s in various fields. Rarely is anyone ever awarded the Ph.D. from the asphalt jungle and is around to tell about it. Mr. Gholson said *"living in the midst of pimps, prostitutes, drug peddlers, robbers, cut-throats and bandits, was rough."* He rode the crest of a pimp's success for 40 years and survived through it all.

Today he says, *"he has nothing material wise to show for his efforts, only memories."*

He says, ***"thanks for the memories."***

--- *by: Mr. Alfred "Bilbo" Gholson*